CAMBRIDGE LIBRARY COLLECTION

Books of enduring scholarly value

History

The books reissued in this series include accounts of historical events and movements by eye-witnesses and contemporaries, as well as landmark studies that assembled significant source materials or developed new historiographical methods. The series includes work in social, political and military history on a wide range of periods and regions, giving modern scholars ready access to influential publications of the past.

A Farmer's Life

George Sturt (1863–1927) was a British wheelwright and writer who usually wrote under the pen-name George Bourne. A native of Surrey, he inherited his father's workshop in the rural village of the Bourne, near Farnborough in 1894. He began to record the daily lives and recollections of his rural family and acquaintances, which he published towards the end of his life. First published in 1922, this volume contains Sturt's unique biography of his uncle, farmer John Smith. Sturt bases his account of his uncle's life around Smith's anecdotes and recollections as recounted him during the last years of Smith's life. This unusual structure provides a lively, intimate account of the life of a farmer in rural England during the nineteenth century. Through Smith's recollections and Sturt's own memories, Sturt sensitively describes the domestic life, work and farming methods of a now vanished way of life.

T0370949

Cambridge University Press has long been a pioneer in the reissuing of out-of-print titles from its own backlist, producing digital reprints of books that are still sought after by scholars and students but could not be reprinted economically using traditional technology. The Cambridge Library Collection extends this activity to a wider range of books which are still of importance to researchers and professionals, either for the source material they contain, or as landmarks in the history of their academic discipline.

Drawing from the world-renowned collections in the Cambridge University Library, and guided by the advice of experts in each subject area, Cambridge University Press is using state-of-the-art scanning machines in its own Printing House to capture the content of each book selected for inclusion. The files are processed to give a consistently clear, crisp image, and the books finished to the high quality standard for which the Press is recognised around the world. The latest print-on-demand technology ensures that the books will remain available indefinitely, and that orders for single or multiple copies can quickly be supplied.

The Cambridge Library Collection will bring back to life books of enduring scholarly value (including out-of-copyright works originally issued by other publishers) across a wide range of disciplines in the humanities and social sciences and in science and technology.

A Farmer's Life

With a Memoir of the Farmer's Sister

GEORGE STURT

CAMBRIDGE
UNIVERSITY PRESS

CAMBRIDGE UNIVERSITY PRESS

Cambridge, New York, Melbourne, Madrid, Cape Town, Singapore,
São Paolo, Delhi, Dubai, Tokyo, Mexico City

Published in the United States of America by Cambridge University Press, New York

www.cambridge.org
Information on this title: www.cambridge.org/9781108025256

© in this compilation Cambridge University Press 2010

This edition first published 1922
This digitally printed version 2010

ISBN 978-1-108-02525-6 Paperback

❡ Of this edition of *A Farmer's Life* have been printed 750 numbered copies only for sale.

❡ Copy Number

A Farmer's Life

COLEFORD FARM

A FARMER'S LIFE
WITH A MEMOIR OF THE FARMER'S SISTER
BY GEORGE BOURNE
THE ILLUSTRATIONS CUT ON
THE WOOD BY STEPHEN BONE

JONATHAN CAPE ELEVEN GOWER STREET
LONDON MCMXXII

By the same Author

THE BETTESWORTH BOOK
MEMOIRS OF A SURREY LABOURER
THE ASCENDING EFFORT
CHANGE IN THE VILLAGE
LUCY BETTESWORTH
WILLIAM SMITH, POTTER AND FARMER

First published 1922

Printed in Great Britain by R. Clay & Sons, Ltd., Bungay, Suffolk.

Contents

Chap.		Page
1.	*Welsh Cattle*	17
2.	*Dog-Traction*	23
3.	*The Country Flavour*	30
4.	*Tramps*	39
5.	*" Smith "*	44
6.	*Surface Water*	50
7.	*Obstinacy*	58
8.	*Oddities*	62
9.	*Farnborough Recalled*	70
10.	*Two Harvesters*	75
11.	*The Bachelors*	84
12.	*At the Farm*	93
13.	*Chiefly Thatching*	102
14.	*Retiring*	109
15.	*Retirement*	115

vii

Contents

Chap.		Page
16.	Mr. Smith's Chatter	121
17.	More Chatter	131
18.	Ebbing Powers	138
19.	A Rally. 1 : Mr. Smith's Manner	142
20.	A Rally. 2 : Conversation	148
21.	Collapse	160
22.	Souvenirs	166
	Ann Smith	177
	Appendix	202

List of Illustrations

		Page
Coleford Farm	Frontispiece	
"Tumbledown Dick"		27
Canal		35
Road		53
Old Farm		79
Interior of Cow-sheds		97

Preface

THE details in the main part of this book —namely, in the first part, relating to my uncle John Smith—are derived from notes or memories of my own close intimacy with him, when he was getting on in years. I saw him often; and in him, others assured me, I might see what earlier generations of our family had been like. Yet, much as he may have resembled his forefathers, he had his own individuality; by which I mean that he was always sincere with himself. If he fancied he liked anything his father and mother had liked, it had to win his own approval too, or it had no chance with him. Probably even this was an hereditary trait; probably he was in nothing so much like his father as in a certain unbending attitude in which, with all his amiability, he never departed from the convictions he had proved, the behaviour he had adopted, for himself.

And being thus faithful to his own views, which presumably were those of his childhood, traditional in his ancestry, John Smith was, it

Preface

seems to me, truly representative of a type once very important in England's life: the type that kept the country steady during all the upheavals of the last hundred and fifty years. Modern science is at last dislodging even English farmers, perhaps; yet there is good ground for expecting that the national temper will presently strengthen itself in modern science and make more John Smiths.

Similar conclusions have been reached in another way. During the completion of these chapters a notable change came over my attitude towards their subject. For whereas, at the start, it seemed that they were justified by something exceptional in John Smith, on the other hand, before the end was reached I realised that the exceptional thing was my intimacy with such a man, allowing me to see a little inside him, rather than in any great difference between him and his fellows. I knew him better than I knew them— that was all. In the course of many years I must have met dozens of men who would have been as good to know, if only I had happened to be equally well acquainted with them.

This does not at all mean that John Smith was less worthy of attention than I had thought; on the contrary, it makes him seem more and more worthy. Instead of being a rarity he was a type; instead of displaying singular and therefore unim-

Preface

portant characteristics he was a mirror, a glass, in which ages of England's life could be seen and loved. To know him was to know the sort of man Shakespeare knew, " whose thews were made in England "; and it was a continual enrichment of the whole outlook when, thanks to John Smith, I was more and more able to appreciate the time-honoured sturdy life still going on in every other farm throughout the southern counties. Verily the English were no parvenus! During centuries of silent and good-tempered endeavour just like my uncle's, there had been a give-and-take of character between them and the heaths, them and the pastures and streams and hills and woods and trades. I began to feel (and that was better than knowing intellectually) the meaning of the lanes and hedges, the crops and hamlets. Through long ages men like John Smith had willed to have these things so.

Yet it must nowise be thought that this uncle of mine had no singularities of his own. Of all the farmers I have known he was perhaps the least grasping; not so much because he did not care for money, as because he cared for other things more. His duty to his fields fascinated him. He showed also what seemed to me an excessive zeal for his landlord's interests. So, one way and another, he never made money, never kept his gig; but was respectable in a less showy way. He was no great frequenter of markets; still less of market inns.

The reason for this may have been partly that the customary sociability of markets did not quite suit either his pocket or his taste. His pocket, never too well lined, might very well not have afforded such a hole in it as " treating " must have cost jollier men every week. To many men the markets of Farnham, Alton, Petersfield were a sort of farmers' club, where boon companions were sure to be met and where the gossip of the countryside could be jovially exchanged; where men whose field-life was often solitary could enjoy the company of their equals. Inns did good business; their parlours got crowded with friends smoking, drinking, settling bargains, swopping yarns.

But John Smith, even had he had shillings enough for this sort of pastime, was still a little bit too reserved to like it. He never swore; he never told a " smutty " tale. He would have been slightly out of his element in the ordinary market inn; in short, he was by way of being a trifle straight-laced. Others there were indeed as punctilious; but these others wrapped themselves round in aloof dignity which had an air of pride in it quite foreign to John Smith's manner. His religion was, I should say, more heart-felt than most men's; there was a glow of sincerity

Preface

in his outlook, conventional though he was in all
his views. But at leaſt he never played the
superior person.

Yet what a high-minded race they were, if in
some cases rather purse-proud—these provincials,
of whom Mr. Smith, whatever the poverty of his
purse, was essentially one! It is pleasant to think
of them—the Simmondses and Mulfords, the
Hewetts, the Bakers, the Cranſtones, and dozens
more—men shrewd sometimes to the point of
avarice, yet of unimpeachable integrity. Their
word was their bond; they were touchy on a
point of honour; in their sunburnt faces, and
through their nutty vernacular, the gorgeous
English countryside seemed to live and speak,
and they were worthy of it.

Such were the countrymen I knew, and such
was John Smith in the main features of his
charaĉter. His very defeĉts were noteworthy,
because with the qualities they came from they
have such a place in the career of the English.
If he was at times over-prudent and always over-
anxious; if he never let himself go in company
and never was reckless and gay, it was for reasons
that had produced Wesleyanism, Quakerism,
devout churchman though he was. A sort of
inſtinĉtive spirituality lurked for him round every
corner. He never got on glad, confident terms
with it: even in his youth (I surmise) it had

xv

inspired him as with an old man's seriousness.
He was not afraid of death but a little timid of
life. Somehow, more than moſt men I fancy, he
felt the vaſt processes of Being going on around
him; and they filled him with awe. And this
too the English fields have had a trick of producing in country folk here and there, through
many generations.

Chapter 1 *Welsh Cattle*

IT has been told elsewhere how the little boys at Farnborough village school rather liked to be naughty at certain seasons and made to stand on the form, because from the form they could look out of the window and see anything that passed along the road. Such a season, especially, must have been the few days before and after Blackwater Fair—the 8th of November; for then the roads, those elm-lined Farnborough roads, usually so quiet, were lively with frequent herds of Welsh cattle going to or from the fair.

It was doubtless a sight well worth being punished for. Long years afterwards I too—though with none of the luck of the Farnborough boys (my education was neglected: I never went to a school where they stood on forms)—used to wonder at the multitudes of cattle, going from Blackwater then to Farnham Fair on November the 10th. Smallish black beasts they were, if I remember right, with long horns. But for how many ages already, before Farmer Smith's time, Welsh cattle had been a feature of Blackwater Fair I cannot even conjecture. Mrs. Piozzi speaks of cattle at that fair, in her Italian travels; earlier still (August 17, 1763) Wesley had crossed the New Passage of the Severn, going from Bristol

A Farmer's Life

to Chepstow, in a boat that had brought over " a herd of oxen." It is true he doesn't state where the oxen were going; but, from the month as well as from other considerations, it seems likely that they were on their way across the south of England, and due in the Hampshire neighbour-hood in November. In this connection I had an interesting note from a friend in Gloucestershire one September. The ferryman at Arlingham Passage, he reported, had told of seeing in his youth, in the early autumn, as many as four hundred head of cattle on the Welsh side, waiting to be got across the river. So perhaps Wesley had seen Blackwater Fair cattle. In fact, one must think that even in his day the bringing of cattle from Wales was a very antiquated part of England's life.

Be that as it may, the custom was in full swing in John Smith's young days. He often spoke of it. The subject came up first during a discussion of the roadside ponds of Farnborough. These ponds, it seemed, had not always been useless. For one thing, they were necessary for the travelling herds. Five or six ponds were mentioned—mostly dried up or drained or filled up now, though one remained—Slades Pond. As this was almost opposite Mrs. Cooke's school, one may imagine how eager the little boys must have been to be deemed naughty enough for

Welsh Cattle

standing on the form, where they might look out at herd after herd of cattle.

John Smith said he used to like to listen to the Welsh drovers. He knew when they were coming, to what fair (for Blackwater was merely the greatest, not the only one), and " purty near how many droves they were bringing." They came, never touching the turnpike roads. " They'd lose a day goin' round, sooner 'n they'd pass a ' gate.' " So, right away from the west of England, they worked their way up, keeping along on the commons, towards London. Then, nearing London, they diverged southwards to the sea.

Details to fill up some of these outlines were obtained from time to time. The droves numbered up to a hundred and fifty each, and at certain seasons their passing through the neighbourhood was continuous. November and December were their months, the November passing, for Blackwater, lasting about four days. To Farnham Fair, never much of a cattle fair indeed, not many of the Welsh came. If other drovers found one of their number going there they were careful to stay away for fear of spoiling his market. At Blackwater, on the contrary, they congregated freely. All along the route the cattle were sold out gradually, but the chief market for them was at the coast. Should a drover, however, get rid

A Farmer's Life

of all his stock before reaching the coast, it was
sometimes worth his while to go back to Wales
for more. From Farnborough the way seems to
have been towards Horsham and Brighton—a
fact pleasantly recalled to John Smith when, in
his old age, he at last visited the former town.
For he was reminded then of places he had often
heard of in his boyhood in connection with the
Welsh cattle.

Ten miles a day was about the journey for a
herd, across commons, avoiding roads excepting
for roadside ponds. To know these ponds, and
to arrange for reaching them at a reasonable
time, was of course an important item in a drover's
business; and of course, too, he needed to know
how the commons followed on. The latter
were wanted only for travelling over; for feed,
arrangements had to be made with farmers, to
allow the droves a turn-out in the pastures. At
nightfall the cattle arrived at a pasture, to rest
and to feed; but often the next evening would
have come (such was the drovers' policy) before
the herd was on the move again, for a shorter
stage to be done by night.

All these arrangements, plainly, needed to be
planned out beforehand; and if it was profitable
to the farmers to sell their feed, the Welshmen for
their part were shrewd at bargaining. " Upright
men," John Smith found them, " but close-fisted."

20

Welsh Cattle

He always got along comfortably with them; only sometimes it annoyed him when "four or five, or as many as six at a time," would come to bargain with him, talking in English as good as his own, and then suddenly turning to one another to gabble in a tongue he couldn't understand. He felt at a disadvantage then.

With every herd there were four or five men on horseback—often two on one horse. And all up the main roads were the known inns—their customary places of entertainment—where a clever landlady was needed to satisfy these welcome guests, and a clever cook to keep the frying-pan going, for their food. Fried liver and bacon was a frequent dish with them.

Of these men one, William Thomas by name, had a reputation for shrewdness, even amongst his own fellows. He was an owner rather than a drover. He would ride three or four days in advance of his herd, buying up the feed; or sometimes he fell behind, to sell again for some other herd a piece of feed his own after all had not needed. He made considerable profit, John Smith thought.

Although the commons were turfy, and the roads—where touched at all—nowise so hard as now, still the cattle needed to be shod, and kept shod, for their long journeys. "Rare fun" this furnished, for a boy. One of the drovers carried

21

A Farmer's Life

a wallet holding a few spare shoes—flat pieces of iron about the length and breadth of two fingers— and a supply of short nails " in a piece of fat bacon." The nails were so kept to prevent rust, so that, if one of them did chance to pierce the hoof, the flesh " shouldn't ganger." (This word was pronounced to rhyme to " anger.") And if any beast showed sign of being footsore, straight- way it was hustled apart, driven over cunningly laid rope that caught its legs, lassoed, and thrown over. And so, with pincers and hammer the shoeing was got through.

It was " the Cattle Plague " (not the foot and mouth disease, but the rinderpest) that finally broke down this custom. For then travelling by road was forbidden and the cattle were sent to their destination by rail.

Earlier in the year—in the autumn—sheep from Wales travelled the same route—" From the Mountains to the Marshes," as John Smith said. They were in flocks of about fifteen hundred up to two thousand, and they came to Blackwater across the commons by way of Reading. A little farther on they were " dis- persed of," to go on, presumably, towards Rye ; " down to the marshes." " Wild as rabbits " they were ; but there were two or three dogs with the men, and " the dogs did all the work."

(See Note A, Appendix.)

22

Chapter 2 Dog-Traction

AN impression of bustling activity, in old Farnborough of all quiet places, sometimes grew out of John Smith's references to the earlier days of his recollection. Not always, of course. When he spoke of the herds of Welsh cattle or of the flocks of Welsh sheep, the imagined sound of innumerable pattering hoofs took the fancy far from bustle to heath-commons and unfrequented roads; and an even quieter glimpse came for a moment, when he happened to mention that he had seen flocks of geese on the turnpike. It was after a remark of my own. I had mentioned to him Cobbett's talk about thousands of geese on the commons between Chobham Ridges and Farnham. " Very likely," John Smith assented. " I remember flocks of them—two hundred at a time perhaps—being driven along the road on the way to London." To think of it is to think of a road where no traffic was likely to be passing for hours. After the slow geese had gone by utter silence would return to it.

But something of a clatter woke up in the fancy—a speedy rattling of wheels—when he told how hawkers were wont to visit Farnborough, in little coster carts drawn by dogs. Leaving a

23

A Farmer's Life

house, he said, the men (in twos, apparently)
jumped into the carts, one each side with legs
dangling over the fore-part. "They would whip
up these poor dogs, and off they'd go—the dogs
barking, the men hollering." Does not Farnborough ſtir in its sleep, at the clamour? The
firſt milk John Smith knew to be sent to London
by rail was conveyed to the ſtation in this way.
A farmer of Frimley had a son in London who
found a good opening; and the farmer took the
milk daily across the Hatches, driving dogs in a
cart "to meet the up train." One of these dogs,
by the way, was "an ordinary house-dog." The
other was a sheep-dog, very savage. "If you
didn't look out he would come at you right
across the road and have you, spite of the cart
and the other dog." The noise of the barking
of these dogs could be heard afar.

But how erroneous is fancy! While I piƈure
to myself the scurry of this dog traffic, the true
objeƈtion to it seems to have been, on the contrary, that it would go too stealthily. In the
prevailing quiet it lent itself too easily to mischief,
keeping quiet itself.

For according to John Smith, a couple of men
driving dogs in a light cart could go oſtensibly
hawking cheap goods, but aƈtually thieving.
Their method was simplicity itself. While one
of them was "driving his bargain at a house

Dog-Traction

with the wife or daughter or the maid-servant,"
the other would be prying about. And at night,
when they returned to London or to Reading,
it was with "something else than ware." In
fact, the quiet movements of the dogs, and the
narrowness of the carts, made this mode of travel
only too convenient for robberies. It was easy
to pass the turnpikes, easy to get along narrow
pathways through shrubberies or plantations.
And this, it was suggested, was the reason why
traction by dogs was at last stopped about 1854.

Something a shade more commercial, a shade
more methodically bustling therefore, centred
round the " Tumbledown Dick "—that notable
posting inn. The stage-coaches stopped there,
and not the stage-coaches only. Road waggons
—those cumbersome predecessors of the modern
goods train—were wont to call at the " Tumbledown " on their lumbering journeys between
Southampton and London.

Accordingly, once a week if not oftener, this
was the scene of a fish-market for Farnborough
and the neighbourhood. There, where heath
verged on village, fish from the sea could be
profitably unloaded, and there whoever likes to
imagine it may imagine some slight weekly
clamour, as from a fish-market. Yet the only
detail I can give in connection with this traffic
seems to restore the old country quiet. A hawker

25

A Farmer's Life

there was, Ben Fry by name, who bought fish at this " market " at the " Tumbledown Dick," yet is said to have hawked it about Farnborough, in a cart, three days a week. Perhaps it is well not to imagine the fish on the third day. But it's not amiss to imagine the quiet roads and lanes, and Ben Fry's voice sounding along them.

The " Tumbledown Dick " was probably a place of more consequence then, before railways had brought London so much nearer. Important property sales were held there. Before Aldershot Camp and town changed all the neighbourhood it must have been the last house on the road for miles. In John Smith's childhood, he dimly remembered, the old sign showed a man in top-boots, with pipe and glass, falling under a table. Soon after Aldershot Camp was founded an officer there contrived to get this altered to a painting of a hussar falling from his horse ; but later this was replaced by an attempted reproduction of the earlier picture. John Smith used to attend the property sales at the " Tumbledown," not as a buyer—he never had any money for that. But as an inhabitant of the district he felt a need to know the values and the ownership of lands and houses. Several old sale-catalogues, marked in his writing with names and figures, are indicative enough of business interests, business chatter, in thin trickle of loquacity hovering about the ancient

"TUMBLEDOWN DICK"

Dog-Traction

inns and roads and home parlours—where, of course, all details came to be talked over at last.

Yet after all it amounts to nothing. The dogs and their carts might rattle across the village, the slow waggons from the coast might encourage a weekly fish-market; farmers might congregate, with loud sapient voices, at the property sales at the " Tumbledown Dick "; but with it all Farnborough remained incurably quiet in its surrounding heaths. Listen to this—a stray reminiscence of John Smith's.

When the farm horses, he related, were at a contract at Heatherfield Nursery, he was wont to go, of a summer night, on to the mound behind the kiln at the pottery; and from there he could hear the horses, three miles away. As I have heard others tell similar things it isn't necessary to attribute exceptionally good hearing to John Smith. But it is well to remember how quiet the summer nights could be in Farnborough, when horse footfalls could be heard three miles away.

Chapter 3   The Country Flavour

JOHN SMITH was so much a man of the countryside it is worth while to try imagining what that country was like which was the scene of his life and gave a flavouring to his talk.   In his boyhood and young manhood, in the days before railways, were the lanes muddier, the roadside trees less tall, than in my own memory ? Was the winter more wintry then than now, colder, wetter, gloomier ?   Certainly winter preponderates in my fancies of old Farnborough.

This is, no doubt, partly due to picture books of that period—pictures full of snow and lowering clouds, of men in heavy overcoats and of stage-coaches stuck in snow-drifts, of leafless trees, and shivering animals, and so on.   It is a rugged England, with rugged people ; a country which, maybe, George Morland composed for me— Morland interpreted later, perhaps, by the author of *Lavengro*.   But I suspect that John Smith himself was partly responsible.   A weather-beaten man he was.   You could see he had lived a strenuous outdoor life.   And as his hair grew frostier and he liked the fireside better—pulling off stiff and ponderous farm-boots to dry in the fender—it added to his comfort to recall the

The Country Flavour

discomforts of earlier days. Better than his grog this pleased him. Indeed, save for the feeling of company, he was not much of a one for grog; nor yet could he smoke; but he delighted to sit and let the old memories trickle out of him. And, though he didn't at all intend it, being no grumbler, his memories did often suggest hard weather. Unawares the hints dropped from him; he didn't mean it, but couldn't help it. Still less could he help the additions with which my own imagination eked out what he told.

As an example—in fireside chatter about the turnpike roads he mentioned a series of clumps of fir trees by the wayside—by Laffan's Plain, I think. And he told how those trees had been planted there to indicate the road in the event of deep snow. No doubt in memory he visualised the very district. But he didn't describe it. It was my own fancy that furnished a wide snow scene, a desolate country, a track doubtfully marked out by dark tree-tops just high enough to show a line of inky blots across the white waste. John Smith, however, must have seen something of this sort with his own eyes.

Another time it was not snow but pitiless winter rains that had to be thought of to explain the objects of his dreamy memories. He was telling of one Smithers, who drove the mail-cart from Bagshot to Farnborough, calling on his way at

31

A Farmer's Life

the Frimley cottage where little John Smith was at school. A big, good-tempered, round-shouldered man was this Smithers, well liked by the children. Seeing him coming, in his queer rattling little cart, the children would run up with a " How do, Mr. Smithers." And John recalled that the mail-driver's overcoat had " ten or a dozen tippets." But, hearing of this protection, who could help thinking of cold rain and searching winds across the heaths? If Mr. Smith did not, himself, recall the downpours met with in the mailman's daily drive, they streamed through my own fancy when he described the driver's coat.

Another time clear and sunny frost was what I got. It had been his duty, as a young man, to drive to Pirbright Mill with wheat, for which he would return after ten days, taking a second load and bringing home the first converted into flour. And in the winter, when he came in sight at top of the hill, the miller's wife would set elderberry wine on the fire to be warm at his arrival, this being his customary welcome. For she seemed as glad to give it. . . . And, John added, he could seem to see even now (in his old age, and by his winter fireside) " the old miller leaning over his half-door to watch him coming down the hill."

It seems to me that John may have been

The Country Flavour

particularly sensitive to cold weather in his childhood. He used to sit by the open hearth, on a cricket stool, listening when he was small to his father's old tales, for asthma often prevented his playing with the other children. At nine years old he was so sickly, he told me, that he "had to be led about." It was not thought he could live to grow up. Long afterwards he had curious evidence that folk took this view of him.

For, being a full-grown man, he went one day to the workhouse, to look up an old chap he heard was an inmate there but had been a labourer, years before, on the farm at Farnborough. The old man stood up, and "bowed" to John Smith as to a stranger. But John protested, "You shouldn't bow to me. You know me, don't ye?" "No, sir, I don't know who you be." "Why, don't you remember Farmer Smith of Farnborough, and his son John?" "Yes, I remembers 'em very well. But the farmer's dead; and John's dead too." "Well," John replied, "seein' that I knows you—it don't seem to me as I can be dead."

But however sickly he may have been as a child, and however much his memory of the seasons may have been affected thereby, he threw himself zealously into man's work as he grew up, becoming in temper one with the district and its weather and its people. To the people, as to the

33   c

A Farmer's Life

weather, he turned a resolute though friendly face, keeping close to their essential character, shrewdly judging them all the time, but far oftener liking their oddities than blaming their follies. He himself knew the difficulties of life far too intimately to be in a hurry to find fault.

Although I had known him all my life, he had gone far past the middle of his own before we got into anything like real friendship. By then, his mother being dead, he had finished out the tenancy of the old farm at Farnborough and was entered into a larger farm at Frimley, which in his hands was chiefly a dairy farm. Rushes grew too readily in it : rushes and brake ferns—plainly it had not been long or thoroughly reclaimed from the marshy moorland. The Blackwater ran, or almost stagnated, on its western boundaries; deep ditches intersected it; yet in wet seasons the waterlogged pastures were flooded, and across the few ploughed fields the standing water in the furrows glittered in long parallels of reflection from the sky. Only in hot seasons was the land tolerably dry; but in the summer plentiful lines of feathery trees gave the farm and the whole district a most peaceful look. And John Smith's spirit loved the peace of it. Certainly it was no farm for a fat profit; but it suited him. It provided plenty of opportunities for industrious effort with the soil, the water-courses, the timber.

CANAL

The Country Flavour

He grubbed a hedge or two; levelled an old gravel-pit; converted two wet fields into one passable meadow; and in short, while making both ends meet with his milk, kept his face hard to the invigorating touches of land and weather. This, I think, is how he enjoyed life. He carried on business because needs muſt; but what he cared for was the intimacy his business thruſt on him with elemental things. He loved, nay, he needed, to do for himself as far as possible—to mend his own fences, clear out his own ditches, cut firing for himself, be his own horse-doctor, cow-doctor; for so he received in his own hands, eyes, skin, brain, the messages that come from wood, from water, from animal life. He wanted no one between him and necessity: no shield; no screen; no servant.

At one corner of the farm a house was built for him—the landowner knew his worth; and here I often visited him. Sometimes I ſtrolled with him, across a rick-yard and through various meadows, to chat with him while he brought his cows home to the new cow-ſtalls to be milked. Then came an hour during which he could only talk in snatches, now and then, while I liſtened to the spurt of milk in his pail, or in his son's pail, a few cows away. Wearing a very greasy hat and squatting on a little low ſtool greasy and shiny, Mr. Smith had his head butted into the

37

A Farmer's Life

cow's flank—sometimes clutching suddenly at her leg, to prevent her kicking over the pail between his knees. He couldn't talk much, nor listen much. But it was pleasant enough to look on.

For in summer, with the farm-yard just outside, sunshine reflected, all glowing, into the cool cow-stalls. Flies came buzzing in, with sleepy-sounding hum or sudden invasion; and now and again a swallow in the shadowy roof swept past. The cows munched lazily; their tails flicked; the sound of the milking heightened the impression of peace and of summer. Yet I liked the same scene better still in winter. It was seldom too cold there, where the cows were. And as the lanterns were lit within, and the winter twilight without turned to starry winter night, I felt that I had unawares travelled to far northern lands, or that time had slipped back and that a very ancient England was still hard at work, amongst the flicking tails in the dim cow-stall. For really the old essential things had not changed—could not change; and theirs was the quality John Smith seemed to live in and for.

I used to get it later, from his talk, when he hobbled indoors with me to his fireside and tea. Whether he chatted about his childhood or about yesterday's gossip, always it was as if the very countryside was talking.

Chapter 4 *Tramps*

"I USED to have a little Christian charity about me. 'Twa'n't much; but still, such as 'twas, there 'twas. But I think it's purty well all squeezed out of me by this job."

So spoke Mr. Smith, distastefully. He had been telling me how he and his carter had been subpœnaed (or, as he said, "suffenaed") to Winchester Assizes, in the case of a man charged with robbery and arson. To this man, so long ago as the previous April—eight months earlier— Mr. Smith, against his rule ("never did it but once before"), had given permission to lie down for the night in a shed, ordering the carter to shake out a truss of straw for him. The next day the tramp, with the police already on his track for an offence in Sussex, was at Alton, obtaining by means of a forged order various goods from a local saddler, which he proceeded to sell again. He then tried another county —Berkshire; but was caught at Wokingham, handed over to the Sussex police, and eventually committed to Lewes Gaol for twelve months on the first charge. On the other charges he had been brought to Winchester Assizes, to be tried by Mr. Justice Hawkins.

39

A Farmer's Life

Mr. Smith having with much difficulty ascertained the date of the man's visit to the farm, after all failed to identify him; and the carter also failed. But the man was convicted, and given imprisonment for nine months, to run concurrently with the previous sentence. This was offensive lenity in Mr. Smith's view. He and his carter, whose wages and journey he had to pay, were by some official quibble robbed of their expenses for the two days. Indeed, they suffered more from Justice than from the tramp; yet it was chiefly in Christian charity that John Smith was injured.

He came home from Winchester and was cross. "Grumpy," he said; "I groused about and wasn't fit company for anybody. Well, Sunday I went to church in the morning and sleep in the afternoon, and wasn't so bad; but Monday again I was in a bad temper, and dunno as I ben't now. I did use to have a little charity, but this job 've purty well squeezed it out of me.

"However, Tuesday night, about dusk, I see an old feller come hobblin' up, and I says to George, ' I won't see 'n. You and Jack must deal with he.' (Jack was the yard dog.) "Jack (on his chain) tore about fine. But instead of the man going, George come back to me. ' He got some sheep here for Mr. Bachelor, and can't get no further with 'em. He's come from

Tramps

Guildford, and wants to know if we got anywhere he can turn 'em in.'

" ' I dunno as we have,' I said. However, juſt at that moment Will came in. ' Oh, well,' he says, ' if he can't go no further with 'em, I don't mind takin' 'em along, to oblige Bachelor.' So off he went with 'em. Poor old Will! he did have a job, too. They was dead beat, poor things ; and it took him two hours to go that three miles.''

" But what about the man ? " I asked.

" That's what I was going to tell you. He was a poor old feller—couldn't get no further. You could see he was tired out. His knees seemed ready to give way under him. He'd juſt come out of the workhouse that morning, he said. He'd got new boots on. He told me, ' I got new boots on, and they have give it to me. I thought I could ha' done it ; but I en't the man I thought I was. Can ye give me a lay-down for the night ? ' ' No, dang it ! ' I says, ' I've had too much trouble a'ready with lay-downs. You muſt go somewhere else.' ' I can't git no further,' he says ; ' if you can't give me a lay-down, when I gits out into the road I shall drop.'

" That beat me altogether. If he went out into the road and fell down there, I should have to pick 'n up and bring 'n indoors perhaps, and

41

A Farmer's Life

that would be worſt of all. However, by this time we'd got out into the road together, and by good luck an old fishman come along in his cart. ' Here, maſter,' I says, ' you 'll have to take this man along with you as fur as to the " Ship " at Farnborough.' ' Damn'd if I do,' he says ; ' it 'll take 'n half an hour to git up in the cart.' ' Never mind. You got to take 'n,' I says. ' No, I shan't,' he says. ' Yes, you will,' I says. And by that time he'd pulled up, and I bundled the old feller up beside 'n. And when he'd got 'n up there he was as pleased as Punch, for it turned out to be an old pal of his."

" And what about his money for the sheep ? "

" Well, as I tell ye, it took Will two hours to get them poor things along. Bachelor come out to meet him and says, ' I'm very much obliged to ye, William. But where's the man ? ' Will didn't know : dessay he was along the road somewhere. ' Well,' Bachelor says, ' I'll walk a bit o' the way back with ye. P'raps we shall meet 'n.' So they come as far back as the ' Ship,' and there they found 'n. Somebody 'd give 'n a glass o' beer. Bachelor looks at 'n : Will could see he was fingerin' a sixpence or something in his waiſtcoat pocket. ' Well,' he says, ' how be we goin' on ? I agreed to pay you five shillin's, but you never finished your job. I dunno what you thinks, but this young man here in my opinion

42

Tramps

have earnt some of the money, so I shall give you four shillin's and let he have the t'other.' And he give Will the shillin' then and there; and Will was mad. He purty near give it to the old chap there before Bachelor's face."

Chapter 5   'Smith'

IN his happiest whimsical way John Smith, being then quite an old man, explained to me that all men were once named Smith, but, departing from righteousness, one after another had been obliged to take some other surname until at last comparatively few Smiths were left. He had forgotten, I think (and so had I, but afterwards I turned up my record of the occurrence), how inconvenient he had found it, years previously, to be one of the still fairly numerous John Smiths.

A quite irrelevant interruption by a curate served to heighten my curiosity on this matter by delaying the satisfaction of it. Why was Mr. Smith resting a bandaged foot on a chair that afternoon, when he would normally have been out on the farm? Had he a bad toe, hurt by a new boot two days previously, and now made so much worse by neglect that the doctor had been sent for? This much I heard, and likewise that there was a laugh about the narrative somewhere. But I had to wait for that laugh, and help be civil to the curate, who arrived at this point on a duty visit, Mr. Smith being one of his best parishioners.

The talk at least brought out some sidelights

' Smith '

in the farmer's character; for it was evidently
designed to please him, and I think he really
liked it. He was twice the curate's age, and in
experience beyond measure ahead of the other;
but on the other hand, his sincere veneration for
the Church made him almost meek and mild to
the churchman. The result was funny. The
two talked almost on an equality, each trying to
come the man of the world. The local question
for or against an isolation hospital for the parish
lasted them some time and gave them good
opportunities to be knowing; but, for the rest,
the curate's conversation was innocent and im-
proving. Mr. Smith named a book he had been
reading: *The Prince of the House of David.* " Ah,
a nice book," the curate admitted, " but I don't
know that you can improve on the Bible. I
always notice about those sacred writers that they
are so sincere, and so honest. They don't try to
hide any faults. There's David, for instance—
the best man that ever lived: a musician, a poet,
a good ruler; and yet—his sins are all recorded.
Why, if anyone were to write in that way now of
a monarch I'm sure I don't know what would
happen! But there is so much human nature in
the Bible. We always used to laugh at General
Smith, when he read one of the lessons. He'd
been in the Indian Mutiny and was a rigid
disciplinarian, and did so enjoy some of the

45

passages. 'Let not *one* of them escape!' he would read, fiercely. He was so absorbed in his enjoyment that he quite forgot the people he was reading to. And we always laughed at him."

Then, after excitedly telling how he had bitten his tongue and made it bleed while eating pudding, the curate tried a new tack, exclaiming, " What a dreadful state the French are in. . . . They are so fickle. And it's a curious thing : under the Romans a regiment of Gallic soldiers (and I suppose they were the ancestors of the present French) was placed between a regiment of Spaniards and one of some other race, because it was never certain whether they would fight or run away. And Julius Cæsar, when he came to Britain, makes mention of the uncertainty of the Gauls. Now, Bishop Lightfoot says that the Galatians were a tribe of Gauls who had migrated from the east westwards—no, eastwards from the west—and if you remember, it is for their fickleness that the Galatians are blamed in the Bible. Isn't that a curious thing ? "

From French fickleness he digressed to Zola's *The Downfall*—" a wonderful book ! " ; and from that again to an account of " such fun " they had at Christmas. Did we know a game—kind of charade—you come into the room and act the name of a book which the others have to guess ? Well, at Christmas he had played that game ;

and they had *The Downfall*. " Five of us walked
into the middle of the room and then all fell
down. Oh, it was great fun! And they couldn't
guess. No. But when we told them they said,
' Why! of course! ' " Another book they repre-
sented was *Under Two Flags*, coming into the
room and waving two handkerchiefs over their
head.

He drifted back to books. The Bible was such
beautiful language ; about Queen Elizabeth's
time, you know. Like the Prayer Book. He
knew a man who valued that in a book more
than anything—the eloquence of it. He didn't
care what the subject was, or which side of an
argument it took. All he cared about was its
eloquence. . . . Then the curate told of a bishop
he had known : " such an inspiring man! "
Apparently humorous too. At any rate we were
invited to laugh, and did therefore laugh, at the
bishop's comment on his own arm, swollen with
blood-poisoning. For it reminded him, the
bishop said, " of nothing so much as an elephant's
leg. But the doctor, seeing it, pulled a face
almost as long as a donkey's." Oh, Bishop!
Yet, being assured that he was in grave danger,
his lordship didn't feel afraid. He was a good
man, and kindly, but could say stern things on
occasion. In this he seemed to the curate to
resemble our Lord, who was not always meek.

47

A Farmer's Life

" Dear me! If I told anybody he was a whited sepulchre, I don't know where I should be!"

There seemed no reason why this babble should ever end; but it did end, and my impatience to hear about the farmer's toe could at laſt be gratified. It didn't occur to Mr. Smith to offer excuse for the neglect that had crippled him. He was like any labourer in his attitude towards discomfort. It was all in the day's work. Somebody had to look after the cows and the milk; and if his new boot galled his foot, what did that matter, as long as he could ſtand? These points were taken for granted: he didn't so much as mention them. But to have sent for the doctor? That called for explanation; and he explained therefore, not without a laugh at his own expense.

" I dunno as I should have troubled him," he said; " only a rum thing happened, the day before I laid up. A man come to measure me for my coffin."

" How in the world did that happen?"

" Oh, 'twas a miſtake, of course. The carter's name's same as mine, and juſt before Chriſtmas his old father, with the same name too, come to live with 'n, and—'ſtead of livin' with 'n, he died with 'n. 'Twas his coffin they come to measure for. . . . Well, and then in the evenin', bleſt if they didn't bring the coffin here too.

' Smith '

' No! ' I says, ' I ben't ready yet. When my turn comes, please God I shall be ready; but you take 'n now where he's wanted.'

" And that wasn't all. Let's see, 'twas Monday mornin'. I went to one of the cottages for the rent, and I s'pose I may have been an hour later than usual, what with hobblin' about and seein' to my toe. When the woman come to the door she says, ' Why, Mr. Smith! I be glad to see ye. I begun to think you must be dead! ' ' No,' I says, ' I en't dead yet. But I had a man come to measure me for my coffin this mornin'.' She did laugh when I told her. But I begun not to laugh, 'specially as my foot was gettin' worse. I en't superstitious; but we knows we all got to go some time or another, and this seemed to remind me of that. However, on my way home I called at Sally's sister's, and as soon as she see me she says, ' Oh, you be all right then? I been dreamin' about you all night. I dreamt you was dead.' "

Chapter 6 *Surface Water*

FEW scenes have ever seemed to me comelier in a quiet way than the view of the laſt five hundred yards of the road I usually followed, in going to Mr. Smith's Frimley farm-house. It might be bleak in a winterly north-eaſter, or horribly muddy in any wet season; yet, at whatever time of year, it was always half reminiscent, half ſuggeſtive, of autumnal colouring, autumnal serenity.

As it was old marsh-land, not so very long ago reclaimed, the country lay pretty flat for a long way on both sides of the road. Hedgerows traversed it here and there—hedgerows with feathery-shaped trees in them—ash, oak, an occasional holly. But not much of all this was visible to a pedeſtrian on the road, by reason of the rather higher banks, hedge-topped, all along the way. Here and there a gap gave glimpses of paſture and trees or sour-looking field; but for the moſt part the ſtraight bit of road—a brownish ribbon of colour—was shut in between its own oaks and ash trees, its own uplifted alder hedges. Uplifted, the hedges were, on the boundary banks that had been formed when the deep ditches on either side of the road were thrown out. For note the manner of it. Parting

Surface Water

the farm-land from the road that crossed it were, first these banks, now alder lined ; then ditches as deep as the banks were high—man-deep, ferny, brambly ; and so you came to the road itself between the ditches—the road, so straight, so comfortably safe even after dark.

Yet only the middle of this roadway had been shaped and metalled. A band of turf, ten feet wide or so, bordered it on both sides, and this turf was cut across at frequent intervals, to let the surface water from the metalled way drain off into the ditches. So, when you tried to take to the turf in hot and dusty weather—tempted by the cooler grass and the tree-shade, and wanting to see down into the thicket of the ditches— when you tried to do this, little cross channels balked your steps and (unless you were young enough to skip across these channels) you abandoned the grass edges and took the gravelled road after all.

But nothing disturbed the sense of great peace there. Though so much had, in fact, been altered by man's industry you felt that the trees and the summer and the yellow road and its grassy sides had done it all and needed no more care. There was no scope for further intervention. The spring, the autumn, would in due course renew the beauty of the place ; but man had nothing to do with it. Peace lived here ; peace and quiet,

51

A Farmer's Life

with the dropping acorns, the steady-rustling rains.

This was what I always felt, although I knew it wasn't just so. In point of fact this little stretch of converted marsh, this five hundred yards of English charm, kept strong men active and watchful year after year. If ever they relaxed it was ready to revert to what it had been before England was settled. The spring and autumn, the rains, the trees, the grass, the dust, all had still to be managed as by resolute colonists.

One brief episode in this endless effort was related by John Smith, himself the chief actor in it for the time. To understand his part, a certain detail in the locality I have described should be considered a little more closely. That lovely stretch of road, where it touched Mr. Smith's farm, had, on the opposite side, a piece of ground that was reverting to wildness. The owner of this piece of ground was no farmer. He seemed to have some dim idea of the more modern craze for building-estates which has fallen like an unsightly disease on all that neighbourhood, and he had, in fact, built a sort of villa overlooking Mr. Smith's pasture across the road. The villa was less offensive to the eye than might be supposed. A few scrubby fir trees half hid it: besides, the alders on the intervening bank screened it from anyone passing on the road,

ROAD

Surface Water

save where a gap was cut out for a gateway. A
" ruſtic " bridge across the ditch united the villa
grounds to the road outside.

The bridge was not unneeded. One wet
autumn the neglected ditch below it filled up.
The water overflowed road and bridge too; and
the tenant of the villa complained to the Diſtrict
Council.

And one day, as John Smith was proceeding
to his field opposite the villa, he beheld men at
work pecking up the road.

" What be ye got at now? " said he.

The men explained that they were laying-in a
drain, by order of the council's surveyor, to carry
the waſte water off into the ditch on Mr. Smith's
side of the road.

" Well," says he, " you may go on and I can't
hinder ye. But as soon as you 've laid your drain
in, I shall ſtop 'n up with a turf at my end."

" Then 'ten't no good our goin' on ? "

" That's as you please. But I shall ſtop 'n
up, and what's more, I shall see as he's kept
ſtopped."

But the men had to finish where they had
opened; so they went on with their work,
promising, however, to tell the surveyor.

Some days later Mr. Smith met the surveyor
on the spot, and was civilly queſtioned : " What's
your objection to this, Mr. Smith ? "

A Farmer's Life

" Why, that I ain't going to have the water turned in there; and you got no right to put it there."

" But the water muſt be drained off the road."

" It's drained *on* to the road ever since the common was enclosed fifty years ago. And I ain't going to have it in my ditch now."

Two diſtrict councillors were present, and one of them intervened.

" Well but, Smith, it's only in bad weather that the drain 'll get any water at all."

" And it's in bad weather that I got all I can do and more too to deal with the water I got a right to deal with. The ditch ain't big enough then to take the water from my own fields—you can see it ſtanding there now between the furrows. And now you want to put more there."

The other councillor tried.

" Oh, well, Smith, I'll undertake that the council favours you as much as possible."

" I don't want favours from the council or anybody. But I don't want injuſtice either. If 'twas my own land I'd fight to my laſt penny before you should put a drain in there. As it is, I muſt go to my landlord and get him to help me fight. I ain't going to have it. I'm under covenant to deal with the water off the road further down, and now you wants to saddle me with it up here. Why don't t'other man clear

Surface Water

out his ditch across the road? In the spring
and autumn, if there's a robin's or a wasps' nest
in my ditch, the boys comes and tramples the
banks in, and then I got to clean the ditch out or
have my fields under water. Why shouldn't he
do the same?"

But he suspected, John Smith told me afterwards, that his neighbour had friends on the
council.

However, some weeks later it was reported in
the local paper that " the projected drain against
Mr. ——'s property had not been laid, Mr. Smith
having raised an objection. The matter was
allowed to drop."

And the farmer remarked, " I don't much
believe in these councils. It seems to me there's
a bigger set of fools than ordinary gets put on
'em."

Chapter 7 *Obstinacy*

LAW-ABIDING citizen though he was —a devout churchman and, in politics, a steady Conservative—Mr. Smith had no great liking for the local authorities and no inclination at all to sit down patiently under any imposition of theirs that he could throw off. How he opposed the Frimley Council in the matter of a surface-drain has been told. In that case direct opposition was the course he took. I feel sure it gratified some natural stubbornness in him. But with equal stubbornness he had long previously followed a more exasperating policy in opposing the Vestry.

This may have been in the old Farnborough days—the affair cannot be dated ; but indeed it doesn't matter ; for, early or late, he was always capable of standing up for himself immovably though with good temper. What had happened was that, all unknown to him, the Vestry had appointed him Parish Overseer. Whether he was right or wrong in holding that the appointment might not be declined I do not know. Certainly he accepted the office like a lamb, though he had hardly heard that it was his before casuals began coming to him, for orders for admission to the workhouse. Then he realised too well, if he had

Obstinacy

not realised it until then, that the Relieving Officer had left the neighbourhood.

At this point, I grieve to say, my record grows indistinct. I didn't know then, and I don't know now, what duties fall to the various functionaries who were mentioned to me, and it looks to me as if I have got the titles of them mixed. One thing, however, is sure. The season being winter, it was night when the casuals came to his house, sometimes in gangs of seven or eight together—rough-looking people, Mr. Smith said. So undesirable were they that, if he was not in, his wife was afraid to go to the door to them.

Upon this he appealed to the Assistant Overseer, asking for advice, and the assistant said, " I generally sends 'em to the Relieving Officer, for fear of getting my head broke."

" Oh," rejoined Mr. Smith, " but I don't mean to get mine broke. If anybody comes to me for an order, I shall give him one."

And that was what he told his wife to do.

" I'm afraid to go to the door," she said.

" You needn't be," he replied. " When you go to the door, take an order in your hand. Then ask how many of them there are, and shut the door again while you come back and fill up the order."

The plan worked admirably, for Mr. Smith. But the Vestry were amazed, indignant, finally

A Farmer's Life

held a special meeting about this outrage and called him over the coals. I don't know what they were not going to do to him.

" But," he said, " I thought you appointed me to grant relief ? "

" Only when you think it a necessitous case," they urged.

" But then you makes a Judge of me as well as Overseer ? You've put me into the position to grant orders, and I shall grant 'em. I shall take the application as a proof of necessity. If I found a man asleep on my farm I should send to the police ; and if he was found asleep in the road it would be the duty of the police to lock him up. So what else are they to do but come to me for orders for the house ? "

It is not recorded how the Vestry answered this argument ; but they soon relieved Mr. Smith of his troublesome office.

The hardships of poverty, meanwhile, were slow to touch his imagination. I found it shocking, one winter, to hear him fairly gloating over the unemployment of that season. When told that the railway company were adding to the local distress by stopping one of their ballast trains, and that many of my neighbours were therefore thrown out of work, he only commented, resentfully, that it would do the working classes good. They wanted teaching their place. He

60

Obstinacy

was certainly embittered. For he complained, " I 've got three months' work for a man hedging and ditching, but I can't find a man capable of doing it, and it'll have to go undone."

Yet the " place " he wanted the working classes taught was industrial and economic, not social. If they would do their work at a wage he thought its market value, he by no means wished for servility from man or woman. One day, as we were walking along together, a smart housemaid came from a villa and tripped along the pavement in front of us. Her cap and apron looked most becoming, but Mr. Smith viewed them with disfavour. " Don't that look to you like tyranny ? " he said, as if rhyming the word to " irony," and leaving no doubt of his dislike of the class distinction that resulted in uniforms for servants.

Perhaps villa folk anyhow were objectionable to him in all their ways. Their houses spoiled the country he cared for; their railways had demoralised the working folk ; their new-fangled councils were a nuisance ; they themselves, with all their airs, knew nothing of the country. Obstruction to them was a man's plain duty. And therefore Mr. Smith was pleased to approve highly when he heard from me how a local footpath which sundry villa-folk wanted to include in their own gardens was saved to the public after all.

Chapter 8 Oddities

ALTHOUGH he never seemed to seek for such things, Mr. Smith so often turned up odd memories of odd people as to give the impression that he muſt have met more than his share of queer folk in his time. The charaƈters others read of in novels seemed to have shown themselves off more vividly to him; he had seen them in the flesh. That was the impression he often gave. Yet, in faƈt, it may have been his own whimsical humour that sought and found peculiarity in persons whom others found quite ordinary and dull.

It is, indeed, juſt possible that, in his memories of an earlier era, truly comical glimpses did arise from the clash of older ways againſt newer ways. Thus it sounded quaint to hear, though it is not very quaint to repeat, about that old lady—" Old Nanny," he called her—who took a train journey when trains were new things. Very adventurously—she muſt have been almoſt flighty—Old Nanny aƈtually travelled by train all the way from Farnborough to Blackwater— three miles or so—soon after the South-Eaſtern line had been opened in that neighbourhood.

Oddities

But she said, " Never no more! I never was so hustled and bustled about in my life! "

Not often perhaps would it have been so easy as in this case to assign a date to Mr. Smith's teeming tales; yet often they had the air of old times hanging about them, like the reek of his father's pot-kilns—a scent as of Farnborough village long ago. Oftener still his anecdotes were suggestive of that disagreeable transition period when the whole neighbourhood was demoralised by unsocial influences from the newly formed camp at Aldershot. Men without conscience or appreciation of old country interests —cunning, unscrupulous, selfish men, unrestrained by any public opinion—made haste to grow rich in all sorts of pettifogging and ignorant ways, which John Smith saw and remembered years afterwards.

For example, there was a usurer he spoke of, quite typical of that time, though neither his name nor his habitation was told. The man cannot have been a member of the old village; yet again, rogues nowadays dare not be quite so crude in roguery as he was—it doesn't pay well enough. He dates from the transition. He was just the sort of man of whom the Aldershot district attracted too many, when there was as yet no firmly established social life to put any curb on them. This is what Mr. Smith told of him.

63

A Farmer's Life

People would go into his room, asking for a loan of money. "How much?" he inquired, in bullying manner. The sum being named (as much as twenty pounds perhaps), a "paper" was roughly scribbled out and put before the borrower, yet not to be read. "Sign that!" said the usurer, and the paper was signed. Then, snatching it up, the usurer would fling down some money. "But I asked you for twenty pounds," the other protested. "Well, you got it, en't ye? I've only took off my interest."

This same money-lender was also something of a job-master. One of his drivers, coming back one evening, was called indoors and told to hand over his receipts. "Is that all?" "Yes, sir, that's all." The master sprang up, locked the door, seized the man's arms behind, and commanded, "Now turn your pockets inside out." This being done, more money came rolling out on to the floor. But before it could be picked up there was the man to be got rid of. The door was therefore thrown open and the astonished driver helped out by a kick behind.

Yet this man's employés habitually paid but little heed to his ways. They were often "sacked." But a passage ran through his house; and the employer, after "sacking" a man at the back-door, would walk through to intercept him passing the front-door and give him orders for the morrow's work.

It may have been from this sort of man that the Aldershot neighbourhood derived that evil character which certainly clung to it for many years. There was a man I often saw—a man of bovine countenance, surly yet suspicious—whom John Smith indicated as a tricky employer— exactly the sort of employer whom Trade Unions, nowadays, begin to keep in order a little in other industries. This man, a " dealer " rather than a genuine farmer, was under agreement to pay his cowman a shilling for every calf born on the farm. But, as calving time drew near, he was wont to turn the cow out to graze on a near heath, and the cowman had no claim for calves that came home to the farm from there. But he seldom saw the shilling, Mr. Smith asserted, even for those calves he did assist into the world.

It may have been because he liked to tease me politically that Mr. Smith once told, too fully, of a certain acquaintance—possibly living even now—who had ratted round to Liberalism on plainly contemptible grounds. Would I know why a certain small but cosy-looking cottage had never been occupied since its completion years ago? It was because the owner had had a dispute with the overseers as to its assessment for rates ; and since neither would

E

yield, the owner had revenged himself by leaving the place empty, so that it paid no rates at all.

But, you see, he was such a stubborn man. A Primrose Leaguer he had been, a most staunch Conservative, until about two years ago. Then, however, the Oddfellows (and he was an Oddfellow), with a dinner at an inn toward, had been refused the one hour's extension of time they applied for ; whereat this one man, this Primrose Leaguer, was deeply offended. He wrote letters to the local papers complaining of " a Tory magistracy," and became a Liberal. Moreover, at a recent election he had walked two miles to vote for the Liberal candidate.

But often Mr. Smith's anecdotes of queer people belonged to the older days—his father's days—before Aldershot had been heard of, while Farnborough was still a little lost village, interested in its own affairs and caring nothing for national politics. Yet first for an anecdote that seems to have no bearing upon either period. It tells of the origin of a certain building now used for an asylum. A man called Worthington Castle or some such name began it, to be a residence for himself. His ambition was that it should have as many rooms as there are weeks in the year, and as many windows as there are days. The bricks were made on his own estate and he employed only one bricklayer. This

Oddities

man, what with waiting for bricks and with his own absences, months at a time, for boozing, hardly got round one course of bricks in a twelve-month. Yet he muſt have persiſted patiently; for after many years the walls were high enough for the window-sills of the ground floor. At this ſtage, however, Mr. Caſtle died. To every-one's surprise, it then came out that he had been carrying on entirely on borrowed money. The unfinished building was sold to the truſtees of the asylum.

In some ways Mr. Worthington Caſtle was aſtute enough. It was his wont to drive about with his bailiff in an Irish car; and in the course of a morning's drive he would call at four or five public-houses and have a " ſtraight quart " brought out to him. The quart pot was always handed over the car to begin with for the bailiff to have the firſt drink, but he never got a second. The maſter, when it came to his turn, emptied the pot.

And now, to get back to the earlier days of John Smith's recolleĉtion : a rich man—an owner of property—was mentioned (but I muſtn't give his name) who married one of three wealthy siſters, and managed the affairs of all three of them. One of these three, dying single, left her eſtate amongſt people so remote from her that they had no expeĉtations of inheriting, and let

67

A Farmer's Life

her death go by unnoticed. But when her will was proved, a year later, these unexpecting but fortunate people went into mourning for her.

Soon after this it happened that another man, being left a widower with a lot of money, married a young wife. When at laſt his own turn to die came, there were plenty of villagers who hoped to benefit, John Smith's father the potter being one of them. But they had reckoned without the young wife. She, the ſtory went (and the old chap's nurse vouched for it), held the dead man's hand so as to make it sign a will in her favour.

" Is it slander to say such things ? " Mr. Smith twinkled, telling me and giving names. " Old Mrs. So-and-so that nursed him didn't mince matters," he added. " She said it openly, and she was in a position to know."

The young wife " didn't enjoy it long," John's siſter urged.

" No," John conceded, " but long enough to make things comfortable for all her own family."

But why tell more ? Apart from John Smith's own dry manner, these tales lose their flavour, and their only use here is to indicate something of the social environment he lived in, and how he wedged himself into it. He was for ever recalling some oddity or other to illuſtrate this or that point in his chatter; and some of these may be told of

68

Oddities

in their place.   Yet they do not much matter for
their own sake.   The people he knew interested
him as his crops did, or as the birds and beasts
he came in contact with.   The contact was everything, though he didn't know it.   Those sharp
touches he was always getting from it were the
salt of life to him.

Chapter 9 *Farnborough Recalled*

ON one of my many visits to the farm at Frimley the smell of weeds burning in the fields seemed to wake up my uncle's brain, as certainly it did my own, to remote memories. To me, the most frequent recollection was of the old house at Farnborough, and especially of the kitchen there with its perfume of turf fires; but my uncle indulged in memories of earlier date. Again and again, throughout one afternoon and evening, they oozed out of him, no doubt set flowing, more than either of us guessed, by the scents floating through the October air. Most of his tales that day have been told already, and must not be told again; but the setting of the talk is pleasant to think over—"the happy autumn fields," and John Smith chatting and interpreting the country like a part of it all, as indeed he was.

The stream of reminiscences welled out first as we came to two antiquated waggons under a shed, at the corner of a field. This shed, with its back to the afternoon sun, gave outlook only upon the field and the high hedgerow right across at the farther side. Three women were at work there—one of them a gipsy girl, said to be "the quietest one of the lot, and a very good

Farnborough Recalled

girl to work." To the pale blouses, dark skirts, and battered straw-hats this girl's scarf added a touch of orange colour, which glowed and burned in the misty October air. The women were raking up weeds which had been harrowed out. Eighteenpence a day was their wage, I was told. Mr. Smith explained that he liked the rake to follow, not to cross, the lines left by the harrow; because, in crossing, the rake would bury the weeds rather than collect them. A young sandy-and-white cat, with tail sportively crooked, was gambolling about in the women's company.

Upon this present-day work, and on two or three corn-ricks under an elm, the shed gave view; but within it stood at rest the waggons, two veterans. At first my uncle said he remembered their being made, at about the time of his father's death, fifty years previously. But gradually, memory growing more fluid in him, he concluded that they had only been done up then; receiving then, perhaps, his mother's name, " Susannah Smith," which, albeit faded, was still on their head-boards. Hers they had become; but they had been originally built for her husband—built for William Smith by my other grandfather, George Sturt.

Each of the two waggons, it was recalled, had made many journeys to London with pots; yet plainly the older one had been fashioned for

71

A Farmer's Life

farm-work. Its bottom timbers were framed in the style which at the time of my visit lingered in Sussex only. Narrow-waisted it was, and the front half of it rose boat-like over the fore-carriage. That shape, however, being inconvenient for stacking pottery ware, had been corrected in the other waggon, only the body of which, as my uncle now bethought him, had been renewed fifty years ago, over older wheels and under-works. In this, the bottom timbers were almost flat and parallel. Both waggons had old-fashioned iron-work—square stays and ribbed strouter-sockets.

I viewed them with some emotion. Their timbers were broken; they were too dilapidated for all but hay-carting and harvesting about the fields; they would never travel the hard roads again. Before my time a man of my own name had built them. I must, as a little boy, have ridden in them myself; I had lately heard one of them creaking over the stubble under a load of sheaves—there still was the loose spoke I had heard creak. But they could not do much more; and, as I looked, fancies of other days grew vivid in me, drifting in with the scent of burning weeds and the pictures of the autumn fields and the women working.

But the waggons must have meant much more to the farmer beside me. He began to tell of the toll-gates on the turnpikes so many years

72

ago. Forgotten summers, long-forgotten winter
mornings, wars one never hears tell of, recurred
to him. Then it was, for inſtance, that he told
how the price of lead rose during the Crimean
War; for in one of these very waggons pig-lead
had been brought home from London for his
father's pottery in that far time.

And from these reminiscences his mind, as
if picturing the heaths the waggons once crossed,
wandered off to the droves of Welsh cattle and
to the drovers with their outlandish talk who
periodically passed over those heaths. He seemed
to see the roadside ponds again; seemed to
dream of the fairs the cattle came to, the far-off
coaſt they reached at laſt.

Gossiping of these old times, we made our way
back at laſt towards the farm-house for tea. Yet
before we got indoors another fillip was given to
Mr. Smith's memories by the sight of pigs
unwontedly roaming about a grass-plot near the
farm-house. What were they doing there? I
asked; and was told that they were a neighbour's
pigs, searching for acorns—so abundant that
autumn. On acorns, Mr. Smith remarked,
pigs would fatten almoſt without other food,
only the diet made their meat " kernelly." The
same food was very bad for cows. It would dry
up the milk sooner than anything. It was also
liable to cause ſtoppage or miscarriage. Inci-

73

A Farmer's Life

dentally he mentioned that some gipsies had received permission to go into his fields to collect acorns; but he didn't say why they wanted them.

But these things he only mentioned incidentally. They served to keep my attention on the subjects at hand; but I think there were other scenes present to my uncle's imagination. Was he not dreaming of his boyhood in old Farnborough, when villagers let their pigs out, to run about the village street? At any rate that is what he told of by and by. Of that he spoke, and of many cognate matters, by his fireside in the evening. The dead times were alive again for him. Or were they so dead after all? At any rate living illustrations of them had charmed my senses all day; for the autumn fields, the smell of burning weeds, the ways of pigs, were not exactly modern.

And so, when at last I left, brimful of anecdotes and country chatter, the centuries of England's life felt familiar, as if only the darkness hid them. Nothing was really gone. Unchanging country interests and affairs hung round. True, I no longer was reminded of couch fires, no scent of smoke took my attention. But, better than that, under the hedgerow trees many rich patches of fragrance came from the oaks or from the acorns under them. The night was not very dark, but foggy and still and moist.

74

Chapter 10 *Two Harvesters*

ALONG the road already described (Chapter 6), between the brambly ditches and under the hedgerow oaks, I made my way from the farm-house to the antiquated farm-yard about a furlong off. As the two places were on the same side of the road—the weſtern side—it would have been a little shorter to cut across the intervening paſture and potato-field; but I liked the road better that Auguſt afternoon. From there, firſt the farm-house, and after it the older buildings, lay off in a haze of glowing weather; the road was ſtatelier than the paſture and field would have looked; and especially it was well to enter the old farm-yard by way of the road. A hundred yards or so of narrow lane led to it—led, it seemed, into the heart of the afternoon—and to traverse that lane was to walk back into a quieter century.

For at the end of it lay the little ſtone-fenced yard. Boulders had been used for its walls; and at the farther side of the yard, looking as old as the grey boulders, were two cottages. One of them was dilapidated, the other had been done up for the carter to occupy. The ſtables for the farm-horses made one side of this yard.

Thither I took my way, discerning, the farther

75

A Farmer's Life

I went, the time and place for a rustic idyll—
for some eighteenth-century harvesting idyll.
The generous August weather seemed to ask for
that.   In the hot sky was just enough cloud to
show immense heights : the cottages and the
grey-walled yard, quiet and nettle-grown, looked
as if they had been prepared and waiting for
generations for something romantic to happen.
Just beyond them was more pasture, more field ;
and near them stood that shed spoken of in the
last chapter, beside the elm and the little rick-
yard.   Only, the ancient waggons were not
under the shed.   They were harvesting.   One
of them, in fact, loaded with oat-sheaves, stood
under the elm.

Farmer Smith himself was in the waggon,
with a prong pitching the sheaves from it on to
an unfinished rick one of his sons was building
there.   As ricks will until they have had time
to settle down, this one trembled at every movement on it ; and it slightly leaned towards the
waggon.   But this seemed not to matter.   Father
and son, and later on the two waggoners, were
well content.   The easy, steady toil told as much ;
and so did some occasional quiet jest or other,
breaking into the silence.   For the most part
only the dry sheaves rustled, and there was
no other sound.   As the waggon-load lowered,
slowly the rick grew to a more tottering height.

Two Harvesters

Another load was brought. It held more than enough to finish the rick. Before ſtarting on it, the four men knocked off for tea and to milk the cows. There was no urgency. The weather was set fair. One more dry day and the harveſting would be over.

After the great glare outside, the cow-ſtalls looked almoſt dim, spite of the reflected light through the open doors. It was pleasant to ſtand liſtening to the continuous spurt of milk into the pails. In one corner of the ſtall was a heap of new hay, moſt fragrant. What a couch! Again the idea of harveſt idylls came to me.

About the hour when afternoon begins plainly to turn to evening we went back to the rick-building, across the paſture and the potato-field, Mr. Smith chatting the while. He was full of praises of the weather : such a wonderful season! All the crops had come ſtrong and clean. The hay had been firſt class ; these oats were good ; and yet, with all the abundance, so splendid had the summer been that no extra ſtrength had been wanted on the farm. " Except," the son reminded him, " two women for hay-making."

Yes, the farmer conceded that. Certainly he had put on two women, and a man—a ſtranger —for a fortnight. But that was all. There had been no hindrances. The good crops had coſt less to gather than many a poor one.

77

A Farmer's Life

The cloud was increasing a little. Vaſt ſtretches of it spread out—if anything higher than ever; and above them again, at an inconceivable diſtance, was another flock of clouds, glowing softly in the unseen sunshine. Indeed, a tranquil evening glow was settling on everything. Especially I noticed it on a waſte patch in the old yard, where a crop of ripe seeding grass swayed carelessly. Once more came the suggeſtion of idyll. Everything was ready; but where was the ſtory?

Towards sunset the rick was finished. A tarpaulin was pulled over the surplus sheaves in the waggon; the tools were put together under the shed. We moved off homewards again, avoiding the fields this time; choosing inſtead the narrow lane. On either side of the lane brambles on the low banks took a metallic luſtre from the tinted evening; and below them, in the dry ditches, brake-ferns ſtood up, tall and expeſtant. I think Corydon and Phyllis should have been there; but in faſt there was Mr. Smith, grey-headed and hobbling, with yet another of his tales to tell.

" I told you," he began, " we had a man here at work for a fortnight. He came on juſt before the haying; and a capital chap he was, too, wasn't he?" The farmer addressed his son.

OLD FARM

Two Harvesters

" Couldn't wish for a better man," the son assented.

" He asked if I could keep him going for a month or two. ' Yes,' I said, ' I could find him work until Michaelmas at any rate.' Because, he said, he'd got a wife. And sure enough, when he come to begin he'd got his wife with him—a strong, well-set-up young woman, quite respectable-looking; and we put her on at hay-making. She and another woman was all the help we had except for him."

" And she was as useful as a good many men," interposed the son.

" Yes. Quiet too. And quite respectable to all appearance. Anybody 'd have said they hadn't been married long. The man looked as right as she did. And they seemed very comfortable and well satisfied. So they ought. He was earning five-and-twenty shillings a week; and I paid her eighteenpence a day ; and let 'em have some firewood, and beer, and the use of the bedroom in that old cottage."

Certainly the windows there were broken out, as I had seen, glancing up. In these warm summer nights it might have been better to sleep amongst the ferns in the dry ditch. Still, as things went, the farmer had been generous. He proceeded with his talk.

" He'd been here a fortnight, and hadn't drawn

A Farmer's Life

all his money on the Saturday. He didn't want it particular, he said. But Sunday afternoon I was juſt dozin' off for a nap, when there come a rap at the door. The dogs barked and I wondered who 'twas at that time o' day. 'Twas this man. He was sorry, he said, but he'd heard from home and had got trouble there and muſt go and see about it. How long would he be away? I asked him. About a fortnight, he said. ' But,' I said, ' the push o' the work 'll be pretty near through then. I'd ha' kep' you on till Michaelmas, if you'd ſtay and help me now.' No, he muſt go, he said. ' Well,' I said, ' of course you do as you like.' So I paid him the reſt of his money, and he'd got his kit in his hand, and off he went and I thought no more about him. Sat down and finished my nap, I did.

" But bless me! When we come to work Monday mornin' I found I'd got the wife left on my hands! However, she didn't seem to take much notice. She said she'd like to keep on. She should take care he never had the chance to leave her again. . . . But the rummeſt part of it all was that the very next day the man went and took a job for three or four days for my neighbour here, not two mile away. And he've been working for one or another ever since— never more than two or three days at a time.

Two Harvesters

And I'm certain he ain't getting the money I'd have given him."

" Never went out of the parish at all, then ? "

" Never left it. And I met 'n the other day and he says, ' Good evenin', master. I shall look you up again next year.' "

" But the woman ? "

" She went off when the haying was over. I asked her how she was going on. Oh, she said, she'd put by enough to pay her railway fare, and she was going to her own home in Shropshire."

That was all. I had got my idyll, then. But somehow it was not altogether satisfying. For one thing, there was too much railway in the end of it; and something of an earlier era would have been more appropriate to that season and that scene.

Chapter 11 *The Bachelors*

THE Mr. Bachelor mentioned in an earlier chapter as owner of some sheep on the road, figures in my thoughts as a product of the more uncouth side of the village life of Farnborough from which John Smith escaped in his childhood. Bachelor, for his part, never escaped, or only a very little way. He was a survival; and, I think, he himself felt it. So far as I remember he never heartily laughed. Always he had the air of a man who knew that the world was leaving him behind—a deprecating yet rather defiant air; and in sheer excess of honesty he seemed to avoid any pretence at the refinements he dimly perceived in others. It was really a first-class man you saw, if you could see through the half-civilised surface; but this last he was careful you should not miss. He would rather you thought too ill of him than too well. That, at any rate, was my own impression of him; and it was greatly strengthened by seeing how he was always treated or spoken of with respect by my uncle John Smith. Mr. Smith never behaved to him as he behaved to another neighbour he once brought with him to see some new machinery of mine. This other man—a farmer, who always appeared

The Bachelors

in need of blood-letting, so plump he looked—
was smitten by the sight of a grindstone run
from a gas-engine. Such a chance was not to
be missed: Mr. Smith's friend pulled out a
substantial clasp-knife and proceeded to grind
it, while we waited, looking on. But then,
to try his handiwork, the farmer-friend passed
his plump thumb over the knife-edge, and immediately fetched blood. His look of amazement
was certainly funny; but Mr. Smith laughed
like a mischievous schoolboy.

So, however, he never laughed at any of Mr.
Bachelor's oddities. If he spoke of him with
impatience, it was always with regard in the back-
ground. And truly Bachelor needed tolerance.
His sincerity was almost perverse. You could
not help liking him, yet he seemed determined
to make it hard.

To be sure he was always kindly to me. Sometimes on market-days he was to be seen along the
street—a shortish, thickish man, with nothing
in particular to characterise him; and then it
was pleasant enough to pass the time of day
with him and go on. Pleasant enough, because
his grey and shrewd eyes looked good-tempered
in his round, unbearded face. Plainly he had
been to the barber's. Short grey hairs on the
lapels of his market-coat showed it. He used
to carry a little ash stick cut from a hedgerow.

85

A Farmer's Life

The nearest thing to happiness I ever saw in him was one market-day, when, with him and Mr. Smith, I went into a market inn, where Mr. Bachelor sat down as if having a really interesting afternoon.

The time was near Christmas. There had been a show of fat cattle in the market, with a prize offered for the nearest estimate of the weight of the prize beast. Here Mr. Bachelor was no longer a nobody. On the contrary, he was widely acknowledged (Mr. Smith told me) as one of the best judges of cattle in the district. And he had justified the opinion of him that very day. He had not won the prize, but his estimate had been right within a pound or two. Others looked upon him with some respect therefore.

There had been betting on the event. It provoked Mr. Bachelor to enunciate a favourite axiom: "A bet well laid is three-parts won." This he repeated, and told in proof an anecdote relating to a tall man—some Mr. X. or other from Alton, whom the company seemed to know. In a Farnham inn, Mr. X. being present, a certain keen hand, also known to the company, had staked a guinea on it that Mr. X. was not the tallest man in Alton. Others, reckoning on an easy guinea, had taken up the challenge, until the keen hand had got five or six guineas laid against him. At last, there being no one

The Bachelors

else, he said, " Well, Mr. X. ain't in Alton at all !
There he sets." And so the keen hand won his
guineas ; and Mr. Bachelor's point was proved :
" A bet well laid is three-parts won." It was
reaffirmed with some triumph ; and all approved.

After that he grew more confidential, telling
Mr. Smith and me, I don't know why, the
country remedies for measles, and for a boil
on the neck. These remedies were so nasty—
that was the measure of their efficacy—I couldn't
even hint at them here ; yet I felt a little proud
to be received into such a man's confidence,
although evidently I owed it all to Mr. Smith.
It was due to Mr. Smith that I also was accepted
as a friend who might be trusted not to be offen-
sively superior.

But Andrew Bachelor kept his best clothes for
the market, and his best manners for the market
inn. I saw him once in his own farm-yard,
where he was wearing a slate-coloured smock-
frock, suitable perhaps for a mucky job in a mucky
place. But the inside of his house I never saw.
There, it is to be supposed, no comfort was
admitted. I cannot imagine that the house
held a carpet, or a table-cloth, or an easy-chair.
An older brother dwelt there, one Silas Bachelor ;
and also, for a time, a sister ; and those who did
enter the house spoke afterwards of the extra-
ordinary gruffness of Andrew's speech when

87

A Farmer's Life

addressing this sister. At her death a stocking-
ful of money she had hoarded was found; and
after her death, the two brothers—bachelors by
nature as well as by name—would not let any
woman at all come into the house. They " did
for themselves " any domestic work that was
done.

The elder brother, Silas, was in fact a recluse.
He saw few people; but he accepted John Smith
into his friendship. Most likely he was more
to blame than his brother for the unsocial habits
of the pair. An odd thing was told of them. It
was their custom, on Sunday afternoons, to go
for a walk; but each always went alone. If you
met one of them, you might be sure that the
other was nowhere near.

Presumably Silas worked on the farm—I
never heard. It was generally supposed that
the two were saving money; certainly they were
living frugally enough. And the idea also came
to me (I don't know whence) that they were also
getting bits of property here and there. Accordingly, when at last their old place was put up
for sale (they had been born in it, I think), everybody expected that they would buy it. About
this time Andrew was reported to be drinking
too much and too often. However, he went
to the auction. But he made no bid. He
heard his farm and his home sold over his head

The Bachelors

and spent the evening at a public-house, heavily drinking. After that little more was told me about him for a long time. He came no more to Farnham market. By and by it was said that he and his brother were under notice to quit.

This state of things lasted a longish time—I don't know how long; then word began to go round that Andrew, the younger brother, was dying. He was probably nearly seventy years old then, and nobody paid much heed. Only John Smith, as an old friend, took or made an opportunity of calling at the house to inquire. He heard somebody come to the door: it was opened—an inch or two, just enough for him to see that it was Silas who had answered his knock; and then, without a word spoken, it was shut again. At that Mr. Smith left, supposing that Andrew must be dead, to account for such strange behaviour.

Near the house was a neighbour named Ship, working in his garden. Him Mr. Smith accosted, asking, " Is the old chap dead, then ? " and related what had happened. " No, Mr. Ship didn't think he was dead. He wasn't dead an hour or two ago, and he didn't think," etc., etc. But of course he couldn't speak quite certainly; so Mr. Smith went home.

That evening, however, or perhaps the next day, a messenger (probably Ship himself) came

89

A Farmer's Life

asking Mr. Smith to go and see the brothers.
For Ship had seen Silas; and " no mistake Silas
did swear and go on, when he heard what he'd
done! If he had ha' known 'twas me . . ."
said Mr. Smith. " But he didn't see who 'twas,
and shut the door."

Of my uncle's visit nothing was told me. But
Andrew died, and my uncle went to the funeral.
The only relative there was Silas. Lonely, Silas
followed the coffin; a man grey-haired, stooping,
feeble, shut in by himself. And so the service
was gone through.

But it was scarce over, and the parson had
hardly turned to walk away, before the aged and
stooping mourner walked to the head of the grave;
and the lookers-on saw a strange sight. Silas's
back straightened, his shoulders broadened; he
stood tallish, dignified; took one glance down
into the grave, then, with longish grey hair
falling down, turned his face to the sky and cried
aloud, " Farewell, brother! May we soon meet
in that better kingdom!"

After that I suppose he went home to his
lonely house.

But Mr. Smith, telling, added, " I never saw
anything like it. And half of them that was
there—they was mostly women—was in tears."

Questions of mine followed—I wanted to

The Bachelors

know especially if Silas had any religious habits. Did he, for instance, ever go to church ? My uncle could not say. He supposed so ; but obviously he did not know. He was, however, reminded of another incident he had heard of, two or three days or a week before Andrew Bachelor died.

One of the near neighbours to the Bachelors had married a certain Milly Wicks. This woman seems to have been one of those gracious souls whom nature forms to be helpful, while sorrow teaches them good sense. Daughter, she was, of a publican—an intemperate man, in whose lifetime she had no comfort. Then, he dying, his widow married again, and again Milly Wicks had small reason to bless fate. Another acquaintance was in love with her, but not she with him. She married a man who took to drink and ill-used her but died soon. Meanwhile the other acquaintance, from being a groom in England, had gone to the United States on a ranche. But somehow the news reached him that his Milly was left a widow, whereupon he returned home, found her, and married her. He proved a tolerably good husband, and, after a turn at inn-keeping, eventually settled down with his wife near to the Bachelors' farm.

To this woman came one evening Silas Bachelor,

A Farmer's Life

begging her to go and see his brother Andrew
and offer up a prayer or something. She hesi-
tated ; but at laſt, pleading that she was busy,
said she would go on the morrow. She couldn't
go that night.

Thereupon said Silas, gruffly, " Somebody
ought to. There, I'll do it myself." And off
he walked.

How the reſt came to be known I cannot
guess. Mr. Smith told that Silas entered the room
where Andrew lay—on the ground-floor, across a
passage from the living-room ; and, leaning
againſt the table, said very gruffly, " Andrew,
do you know the ſtate you 're in ? You en't got
much longer to live, ye know. You 're dyin'."

An inarticulate mutter from Andrew, and then
—Silas again—" D'ye ever say yer prayers ? "

Murmurs, perhaps of denial, from the dying
man.

" Well, ye know," rejoined Silas, " you ought
to. I says mine, and you ought to say yourn."

Chapter 12   *At the Farm*

I N John Smith's young days the site of Aldershot town and camp "was one of the wildest of all our heaths. . . . But it's wilder now," he added, with disapproval. There was a "hamlet" (he chose that word, as more exact than "village"), and perhaps there were as many as half a dozen farms. And he knew, either personally or from his father's talk, every soul who lived in Aldershot. So too of Camberley. Where now are the villas were deep fir woods ; and it was he himself, with his father's horses, who carted the greater part of the woods away. As for that stretch—the Mytchett road and between the two North Camp stations— it was a marsh ; and he had seen Will-o'-the-Wisps where now, at night, gas-lamps glimmer across the still rush-grown pastures.

There used to be an old woman at Camberley so confused in her memory that, although she knew him for John Smith, she mistook him for a dead uncle of his, and he had to talk to her in that character.

These reminiscences oozed from him amidst shrewd talk of more modern affairs. We walked along the road together—he in his shirt-sleeves, for it was a May evening, a Friday. He stopped

93

A Farmer's Life

to pay his carter who was coming from the old farm-buildings, and to ask about the mare, soon to foal. But before we reached her ſtable we came to a gate on the opposite side of the road, and Mr. Smith called my attention to the field within, sown with oats. A neighbour had lately bought it. How much did I guess he paid? What was the extent? Eight acres, he said, and it was probably for building. I guessed £400. "Double that," said my uncle. He discussed the prospects, seeing them from a modern ſtandpoint. So we ſtrayed on, talking of the buyer—a man we both knew and agreed in liking, for all his " nearness " in money matters.

That " nearness " had enabled the man to save money. His father, Mr. Smith recalled, had been a butcher in a very small way of business. " We used to call him ' Old Bramble-mutton,' and ask him when he was goin' to kill t'other half o' the sheep. Because he never killed a sheep unless one got caught in the brambles or something of that kind; and we always said he only killed half a sheep at a time."

I mentioned a recent talk with the son (the Boy Scout movement was juſt coming into favour), when this son told of his own ability as a young man to track a loſt heifer over the heath, reading signs in the heath itself. Mr.

94

At the Farm

Smith was not surprised in the least. "I've no doubt he could. I don't doubt it at all," he said.

Passing along the little lane to the old buildings (may smelt fragrant there), we reached the stable and saw the mare. The carter had come back and stood by—a man with thick, leathery-looking face, nothing of a chin, but wide, good-tempered mouth and clear eyes. Mr. Smith briefly examined the mare ("She's gettin' a big udder," the carter had reported when we met him on the road), then suggested, "Not afore Sunday?"

"I don't think so," the carter assented.

"Well, shift her over presently, and give her a look just afore you goes to bed. And of course if it should be necessary, come for me. But I don't think we shall need to begin watchin' before Sunday."

We went out, across the empty yard—so quiet inside its grey boulder walls—to a big wooden shed now strewn with clean straw "for a sort of lyin'-in place," Mr. Smith explained. One side of it—mere stanchions weather-boarded—had been lately shored-up with limbs of trees, lest the mare should fall against the boards and break them out. All sorts of precautions had been taken. Lastly, the mare, bought for £35, had been insured for one month from the day of

95

A Farmer's Life

foaling. The premium, 19s. 6d., did not insure the foal. It would have cost £3 to do that.

Beyond the boulder wall, on slightly higher ground, was a fair field of rye, just turning into ear. Seen from our lower ground it showed a tender cool green against the evening sky. We leant over a little wicket gate to look at it. " Is the straw valuable ? " I asked. " It should be," the farmer said, " but that shows ye where we are hit. At Aldershot Camp they use nothing but moss-litter now, so there is no demand for straw there. And then, where these gentlemen keep motor-cars " (motor-cars were a comparatively new thing) " they don't keep horses, and there's no bedding wanted for a motor." " And no manure coming from them," I suggested. My uncle assented. There too the farmers were sufferers, he said. Moss-litter made useless manure, and not only at Aldershot Camp but in London too three-parts of the remaining stables were being supplied with moss-litter. . . . I was shown some of the bad hay from a wet summer two years previously. " It ought to have been worth a hundred pounds," said Mr. Smith; " but I'd be glad if anybody 'd offer me ten pounds for it."

As we strolled back across the fields—a small school-boy I had taken with me straying to the hedges after birds'-nests, for was it not May ?—

96

INTERIOR OF COW-SHEDS

97   G

At the Farm

my uncle spoke of his milk-trade and of sanitary inspectors. Lately an inspector had suddenly seized him by the shoulders as he was going a-milking, and asked, "Are your hands clean?" "Clean enough," he had replied, not well pleased to be so disrespectfully treated. And in fact he was overdone with inspectors, mentioning one from Aldershot Camp and two from civilian authorities. He enumerated these, urging that there should be a limit to the number of inspections busy people were subjected to. From that he passed on to explain that pure milk might be as bad as any other, if taken into a dirty home—"in a bottle, for instance, that hasn't been washed for two or three days, and put into a cupboard among old food, flies, boots, and so on. You see," he said, "we that deliver the milk have a very good chance of seeing how people deal with it." We agreed that, as he put it, "you can't make people sensible and cleanly by law, any more than you can make them good."

Here I quoted Bettesworth: "All you can do is to dummer a little sense into 'em."

"And that," my uncle exclaimed, "is where I believe in education, only I don't think they go far enough."

Those level pastures the boy was roaming over, dotted and enlaced with feathery trees and luxuriant hedges, all so tranquil in that May

A Farmer's Life

evening, filled me with a deep content, especially in the company of this man and his country thoughts. I stopped to look over a gate, and murmured, " What a beautiful place."

" Yes," he said. And then, with a sigh, " I wish it succeeded a little better."

The sudden contrast against my own feelings was disquieting. What place was there for commercial anxieties in all this charm? The loveliest peace, the most venerable tasks, seemed threatened by failure. For example, my uncle's potatoes had been cut down by that late frost the previous week. " Ice an inch thick that morning," he said. Besides injury to the crops there was injury to the land. The potato-rows just ready for hoeing could no longer be distinguished ; so, although the couch was coming up thick, the hoe must still be withheld for a time.

So then farmers might never share my own great delight in the weather—any weather—for its own sake? There were always dreadful points of profit and loss for them to consider. The unwonted realisation of this weighed on my spirits, and seemed to rob my uncle's talk of the flavour it should have had to match the beauty of his meadows and quiet fields. I didn't so much enjoy his further talk. But he had no inkling of that, and went on as if nothing had happened.

At the Farm

The evening, the scene, were steeped in so tranquil a look of prosperity as to call up rich memories of other days. Involuntarily we began talking of the old Farnborough home. My uncle's recollections of it were as vivid, he said, as if it were actually before us. He could see it all " as clear as I can see the cow-stalls there now." Every post, every door-latch and hasp— he had them all in his memory. He could not, he said, get the things of to-day so fixed. Take him through Farnborough Park, which had lately been cut up into building plots, and he would be lost.

The state of his memory seemed analogous to that of his sight. Far across the fields he could see now—farther than ever before. At a great distance he could make out the actions and identify the species of the wild birds. But not so well as before could he distinguish near things. Although he could write a letter, he could not afterwards see what he had written.

He himself, to tell the truth, was growing old, while his farming was getting out of date. He didn't speak of it, but I felt it all the rest of that evening. When I came away he walked out as far as to the road with me ; and as he returned alone through his garden I could not help noticing how grey his head looked in the twilight.

Chapter 13 *Chiefly Thatching*

ONE afternoon I took a friend with me—
a man brought up in a Sussex village
—to see my uncle John Smith and the
farm. The weather could not have
been better—the hot and splendid end of July
1906. At Mr. Smith's farm we found thatchers
at work, covering a new hay-rick. It was
pleasant to ſtand and watch them.

Drawing out and ſtraightening the ſtraw
looked an intereſting process. Firſt the ſtraw
was loosened and thrown up lightly with a prong
into a large heap, and pails of water were tossed
over and into it there, making it limp. Next,
from underneath, handfuls were pulled out from
the heap; and by the very aƈt of pulling the limp
ſtraws began to come straight. Being laid out
on the ground, they were then combed out by a
curious motion of the thatcher's hands. One
hand, knuckles outwards, formed a backing or
ſteadiness; the other swiftly drew wisps of
ſtraw towards it with cunning alternate motions
this side and that, the middle of the ſtraws
bending round the well-placed knuckles. Short
pieces and rubbish seemed to separate themselves
naturally; and in a minute there was a big hand-
ful of ſtraw lying ready for the rick.

Chiefly Thatching

But it had to be lifted up without tangling. To manage this, the thatchers were provided with a clutch—an ingenious home-made implement—into which the straw could be packed for lifting. It was made of a forked bough of hazel, cut off short just under the fork and leaving the two slender branches, each about four feet long, spreading to ten or twelve inches between their ends—like a long and narrow V. At one of the two ends a hook was tied with a stout string some six inches long. At the other end was a notch to receive the hook when the two branches were strained together. This thing was stood on the ground, butt downwards; the wisps of straw were packed closely into it; and when it was full the yielding forks were tightened together and hooked, so that all could be safely carried up the ladder.

(One of these implements, ready to " spring " or split down the short connection, had been strengthened there with a fine cord neatly bound round it, as on the handle of a spliced cricket bat, or on those South Sea implements to be seen in the British Museum, in which stone axe-heads are corded into their cleft hafts.)

On the rick the man worked upwards, from eaves to ridge, pushing the upper ends of his straw-wisps into the underlying hay ; but I was unable to see how he gradated the wisps or kept the lower ends from being loose to the wind, or exactly what he did with them at the ridge. Thin, patriarchal old man, weathered, crisp-bearded, plainly he took a pride (my companion drew attention to it) in his work, so neatly did he trim off the top when the ridge had been fixed. A scythe-blade cut down to about half its length made a formidable-looking tool for this job. I could not get to look at its handle; but it was fine to see how sharp the blade was, and how clean and true the old man did his cutting.

He worked standing on a ladder, doing a patch from eaves to ridge as wide as he could reach before he moved the ladder; and when the time came for this he did not descend, but, getting to one side, turned the ladder over and over. This seemed to necessitate that the ladder should lie flat with the sloping top of the rick, and not make any angle with it either at eaves or ridge; and the circumstance seemed likely to be a consideration determining how high the rick should be; but I may be wrong.

It was not possible to me to examine the " spars " that pegged the straw-wisps into place; nor yet could I watch the making of the straw ropes with which the thatch was finally tied down. These had been got ready before my arrival. There were three ropes or " bands " on this rick;

Chiefly Thatching

one at the ridge, one along the eaves, and a third half-way between the others.

Very countrified was the old thatcher's turn-out. (The man helping him was said to be a chance assistant, although skilful to my eye.) Down in the loose hay lay the old man's kit-basket, his coat, etc. A little funny old dog—a brindled cur about as big as a cat, with a lower tooth sticking out and an experienced and determined expression—kept guard. At first he growled as we approached, but afterwards he was quite friendly. A donkey strayed about. Near the rick stood the donkey-cart—a tiny coster-barrow—holding a few more of the old thatcher's things. Late in the evening the old man overtook us on the road, driving solitary and fairly fast. The dog was running under the brambles and ferns, along the dry bottom of one of the roadside ditches, five feet or so lower down than we were.

Mr. Smith was full of praises of the noble hay-making weather it had been. The only real interruption had come about ten days previously, when a rain-storm unexpectedly blew up in the night. The unfinished rick had not been covered with the rick-cloth, so settled had the evening appeared, and about a load of it had to be taken off to be dried again. Mr. Smith had been twitted over this, he told us. In Farn-

A Farmer's Life

borough, when he was going round with milk, somebody asked him, " Did you lose your watch, then ? " " Lose my watch ? What d'ye mean ? " " Oh, I saw ye pulling your hay-rick to pieces again."

At hearing this the man from Sussex laughed. " I've heard that old tale often enough," he said. Down by Findon and Washington, under Chanctonbury Ring, he must have meant. I felt that many generations of hay-making folk had maybe enjoyed that jest.

As we leant over a gate admiring a field of roots (there were cow-cabbages farther on, then more mangold, then swedes) the visitor praised the soil. Then my uncle remembered how he had once sowed wheat there. Many years ago it was, one dry October; and the seed-corn lay in dry dust. An old Yorkshireman passing by had said, " It'll never come up." " That'll be a long time for it to lay, won't it ? " Mr. Smith had replied. A week passed. Then a steady rain fell, and two or three days after it all the drills of wheat could be seen—thin green lines right across the field. In the following August they harvested eleven sacks to the acre there, which was the finest wheat crop my uncle had ever had. Indeed it was a big yield for this neighbourhood. But the visitor with me said twelve sacks to the acre was common in Sussex.

Chiefly Thatching

The cow-stalls, which we had to go into, had been newly whitened inside, I thought. In fact they were lime-washed twice in every year— in May and October; that is to say, when the cows begin to be turned out o' nights, and a second time when summer is over and the cows are brought in to shelter again.

At tea that day Mr. Smith told many details about the old pot-shop at Farnborough which have been included in the narrative of his father, William Smith. Then also I got a word, unknown to me before, but full of a sort of rustic suggestiveness—pea-hacking. Pea-hacking was said to mean the harvesting of field peas. My uncle spoke of a woman he remembered doing this work with sickle as well as fag-hook, and working at it as fast as any man.

He also told of hand-reaping, which was priced at 7s. 6d. an acre, he said. As he was an eager advocate of machinery—perhaps in some resentment still against the machinery riots which had hampered farmers so badly in his boyhood—he was careful to point out how badly the price for hand-reaping compared with that for machine-cutting. For with one horse a man on a machine could cut from five to seven acres a day.

Moreover, if they were any good at their work, hand-reapers wanted to keep on at it and

A Farmer's Life

earn money. They were unwilling to leave off if the weather turned wet; indeed, if stopped they were liable to leave the job altogether. Certainly, where the corn was at all beaten down, hand-workers could cut it better than a machine, which simply goes over it; but their work has disadvantages. For instance, although it has been urged that hand-reaping does not shatter out the corn so wastefully as a machine, on the other hand, if the men do not begin before the crop is ripe, it is over-ripe and will be dropping out before they can finish; whereas a machine may wait until the proper time and then cut all.

So my uncle argued, plausibly enough. Yet it was hard not to suspect him of prejudice. I asked him if there was anything in the assertion I had heard from a peasant turned gardener, that meadow-grass grows better after a scythe than after a machine. The gardener had propounded this apropos of a lawn, urging that the lawn suffered more from the bruising cut of the lawn-mower than from the clean cut of a scythe. Mr. Smith refused to admit it for a moment. But was he right, or was he just a little prejudiced against the labouring man?

The knives of a hay-mowing machine need sharpening every hour, he said.

Chapter 14 *Retiring*

I DO not remember Mr. Smith anything but hobbly on his feet—corns caused by the stiffness of prodigiously heavy boots seemed a sufficient explanation. But as his years increased this infirmity grew more and more noticeable. He plodded along doggedly and with bent back, always at one slow pace; and even so, sometimes he swayed on his feet, and was glad of his stick to help him keep his balance. So, although he never cared for driving, oftener than of old he made use of his milk-cart for distances he would have walked when he was younger. During his wife's last illness, too, he kept a little shabby governess-car for her use, and he retained it for himself for some years.

A drive with him was a thing to laugh over afterwards, though not until one was safely home again. The little old pony he used for his milk-rounds was not quite as slow as himself, but, like him, had but one pace. Frequent flicks with the whip made no impression, or frequent loudish calls to " Goo on ! " The pony paid no heed at all. It was well one had not much dignity to carry; one could not keep it up when driving with Mr. Smith. The

three or four such jaunts I had with him were too
many by three or four. Wayfarers smiled too
openly.

The injury to one's pride was not the worst of
it. If it was painful it was at least funny to be
in such an undignified plight. But in fact it
was a nervous business, cause of much anxiety,
to travel on the road in a cart with Mr. Smith
for driver. It may have been the pony's fault
that, invariably, after proceeding a few yards,
we found ourselves definitely on the wrong side
of the road and stuck to it. Stuck to it, until
something had to be met, or until some quicker
vehicle—motor-car of late years—compelled us
to strive to recover our proper side of the road
in time. But no sooner was the need past than
the wrong side was regained. Yes, it may have
been the pony's fault; but the time came when
I began to feel that my uncle's perversity was the
chief cause of this persistent straying. For it
is more than likely that he resented being incom-
moded on a public road by gentry in a hurry,
and most of all by motor-cars. In a sort of
ineffectual protest he deliberately took the wrong
side. At least he might cause the well-to-do to
feel that they were rather a nuisance.

If that were so (it is only a surmise; he never
hinted at it) his stubbornness was but one more
symptom, amongst others growing daily plainer,

Retiring

that he was becoming an old man. Years indeed were to go by before he was utterly done for—before rheumatism across the hips entirely crippled him. One only saw ruthless change beginning. Old age did not rush upon him in a hurry. On the other hand, it was not quite kindly in its coming. It marred him, if slowly, still pitilessly, because of pain mixed with it—pain, or at any rate increasing discomfort. He was cruelly ruptured. Eczema—a foe for years—fixed upon him at last, and the gin fomentations of his earlier days had to be given up. They were useless after all.

At tea—he liked his tea very hot—he was more and more ready to sit back in an easy-chair by the fire and to have his bread-and-butter handed to him. When he sat up to the table it grew ever more noticeable how bent his back was and how close his grey beard was getting down to the plate. Perhaps I am anticipating a little. Yet there is no doubt that he felt these changes beginning; no doubt, either, that everyone concurred in the wisdom of the step, when at last he decided to hand on his farm to his sons. The landlord willingly accepted them for tenants: the farmer sold them his stock-in-trade at a valuation, keeping only his milk-round, with the old pony and cart, for his own use. That he did not yet give up. He wanted occupation.

A Farmer's Life

Besides, with the proceeds from the small milk-trade, the interest from the sale of his stock, and the scanty pension from a society he had belonged to for years, both ends could be made to meet if he lived frugally; and he wanted no more. On these terms he arranged to leave the farm and live in a semi-detached cottage just across the road.

My last visit to him at the farm, a few days before he moved, ought perhaps to have stirred keener emotions in me than in fact it did. Although I might traverse the fields or look on at the milking again, and even in his company, yet never again would it be with him as master; and it made all the difference. From his own temper (I see it now) a sort of calm—like the calm of a Sunday afternoon—had associated itself in my thoughts with those pastures. He had no notion of it; but comfortableness came from him whatever he did, and clung to his talk whatever he said. For example, his whimsical tones enriched, and endeared to my memory, a brief answer he made when I asked him how he kept his knife so sharp. He was bringing the cows in across his pastures for milking; he wanted a certain fence-rail taken down—it had been tied up with strong string—and he fetched out his pocket-knife and cut the string apparently without effort. How did he keep his knife

Retiring

so sharp? I asked. " Cuts nails with 'n," he said. That was all. But I have often laughed at the recollection of it; not because it was funny —plainly not that—but because it was so agreeable to be there crossing those quiet pastures in company with a man so harmonising with them in spirit as his tones sounded.

But in fact I was never conscious of impending breach in that visit I have spoken of. Something I had lately heard about a family in my own neighbourhood maintaining a parish school long ago was suggestive enough of Mr. Morant's influence in old Farnborough to be worth repeating to my uncle. He pointed out another resemblance: the great house at Farnborough, like the one I had mentioned, had not after all been so imposing as to lead anyone to take it for the Squire's. Schools had come before personal aggrandisement. Perhaps squires had generally taken that view. And this being suggested to Mr. Smith, he at once mentioned other families with an equally honourable record—the Dumbletons of Hawley, the Halseys of Pirbright.

Placid talk like this took up all my time that day, so far as I remember. About Michaelmas —the year was 1906—Mr. Smith, with one daughter to fend for him, moved across the road into the semi-detached cottage already mentioned ; and there he contentedly settled down. He

A Farmer's Life

bought his milk from his sons and delivered it in Farnborough in his own milk-cart. He had an ample garden, which he worked with his own hands—growing roots there for his pony and harvesting them more as a farmer than as a gardener. And he kept a few fowls. One way and another—for he helped his sons at the milking, and for some summers at the hay-making—he always had enough to do, and was glad at evening to slip the boots off his tottering feet. Meanwhile he had for ever slipped off the heavier cares of business, save vicariously on his sons' account. They consulted him many a time, and he behaved to them like an elder brother.

Chapter 15 *Retirement*

ONCE settled into his cottage, Mr. Smith indulged himself a little more in memories of his prime, of his father, and of the far-off Farnborough days. Many details came from him of the pottery and of the clay. He told of the clay-audits he had attended at Farnham; he talked of the Harvest Suppers in the old farm kitchen; he recalled his father's fond visits to many corners of the farm-house in the last day that old man spent downstairs. These reminiscences may have been partly awakened in Mr. Smith by his unwonted freedom from the worst cares of business; he was already an older man than his father had lived to be, and his thoughts in those days were probably drawn often to such comparisons. But there was another thing. In the turn-out of his household goods for removal—though he had no superfluity of furniture—several things hardly thought of for years had come under his notice again, with keen suggestiveness for him. The little rush-bottomed chair used in his father's last wanderings about the house was one of these mementoes. It meant more to Mr. Smith than to anybody else; and he found a place for it now on the landing of the cottage stairs, where

115

A Farmer's Life

again and again it muſt have called up ſtrange, solemn pictures in his memory. He pointed it out to me, asking me if I knew it. But I didn't; so he told me what has already been re-told elsewhere.

Certain details about the old farm led to a talk about thatching; and that, to mention of a family of thatchers somewhat famous in that diſtrict for their craft. Two unmarried brothers were the only survivors then; but Mr. Smith remembered also their father and their grandfather. Generation after generation the family had followed their trade with notable skill; yet, as these two brothers were older men than Mr. Smith—who by now was seventy-three—it muſt have been to their father, not their grandfather, that he chiefly referred.

He had died at work, this man, when paſt ninety years old. With his two sons he had gone out as usual in the cart; and while they were busy on the rick he had silently dropped down in the ſtraw and died. His sons, coming down, picked him up dead and put him in the cart and drove home. It sounds inadequate. Yet what else could they have done?

In his younger days he had been a matchless craftsman, well aware of his worth, my uncle said. Knowing that no other could thatch half as well, he chose not to be huſtled. Did anyone

116

Retirement

try to hurry him (as perhaps some gentleman, insisting, with gentlemanly superiority over one of the working classes, on having his summer-house thatched immediately), this man would begin the work in his own matchless way. So he secured the job to himself: no other could be employed to replace him. But then he went away from it; spent three or four days quietly at the public-house. Not that he "boozed." A couple of glasses in the day sufficed him. He lingered all day over these, however, disdaining to be hurried for anyone.

Of course he had often worked at Street Farm. There, after he had done a day's work, Mr. Smith's mother was wont to treat him to gin-and-water. Remembering this many years later—the old chap was then ninety or so—Mr. Smith on one of his milk-rounds caught sight of him in the village street and beckoned to him. It was just outside "The Prince of Wales," whence two-pennyworth of gin was soon brought out. To this Mr. Smith added some new milk, tipped from the can in his cart. The old thatcher swigged it down and said, "If my mother had give milk like that and lived till now, to this day I shouldn't ha' been weaned."

Incidents like this were not yet quite things of the past for Mr. Smith. Active business he had indeed given up; but he had strength for

117

A Farmer's Life

a sort of pottering industry which kept him still close in touch with his happiest interests. Besides his daily milk-round in Farnborough he was glad to give, and his sons were glad to have, his help at the milking every afternoon. He had but to cross the road to be back again in the familiar farm, and to feel the old life going on all round him almost as if he had never left it. The principal change was that he had cast off the ultimate cares no man in business may evade. Visiting him, I often accompanied him to the farm, and I saw next to no difference. It was a little curious, now I think of it. In the cottage I heard perhaps of doings long ago; and then, strolling across the road, I saw, in more modern life, some illustration or other of the earlier life we had been discussing. It was like living in two epochs at once.

For example, that very day of my first visit to the cottage, the carter from the farm was gone to the parish gravel-pits to dig and bring home gravel for laying down in the farm-yard. Just as the clay on Cove Common (my uncle had been telling of fetching it from there fifty years previously), so now this local gravel was to be had for the getting. And conceivably, if Farmer Smith's sons in after life should tell of their carter going on such an errand three or four times a day, the hearer might think, as I had been doing, how full of incident that old life must have been,

and not at all realise how orderly, how peacefully,
it did in fact go on.

Variety truly there was. The threshing-
machine laft week had left a large quantity of
" cavein's " and " hulls." The latter word I
did not quite catch and I forgot to inquire into it.
But when I asked about " cavein's," what were
they ? my uncle answered, in his whimsical way,
" racketin's." I begged him to tell me in English,
not caring to hint that possibly his English was
too good for me. So then he explained.

" Cavein's " * are the broken ſtraw and bits
of clover which come away from the corn in
threshing. In the old days of the flail a small
quantity was left on the barn floor every evening,
which would be taken up at once and given to the
cattle, who like it much. But the threshing-
machine had left more of this by-produ&ct on hand
than could be used before it spoiled. So Mr.
Smith and his sons, then and there, fell to discussing its worth and speculating who would
buy it. This talk was hardly over when old Boss
Fuller, the rick-thatcher I had watched during
the summer, came along and bought the
" cavein's " for seven shillings.

Meanwhile, in the fields the mangold were
being got up ; the cows had to be milked and the
milk taken away ; nor yet was this all. After
dark, when I was leaving, Mr. Smith's sons

* Note B, Appendix.

A Farmer's Life

could not follow their custom of walking with me towards my station, because they had a heifer likely to calve immediately.

Their father, however, took their place. And thanks to him the older times seemed with me still, as they had done during the day. The night was chilly and dim, with raw land-fog lying across the fields and between the hedgerows, yet not so thick overhead but that the half-moon could be seen hazily above the trees, with an occasional glimmer of stars. But that fog across the road, with the hedge-things standing up motionless in it under the cold-looking moonlight, served to shut out all the modern features of the scene, as viewed by day; and my uncle, hobbling along beside me, gave me a feeling that we were in that earlier time he had been telling of that day. I asked, was it not along there, just where we were walking—just where gaslamps lit what had once been marsh—was it not there that of old he had seen Will-o'-the-Wisp? Not just there, he said, but more to the right, over there by the South-Eastern Railway "Loh," he exclaimed, "what tales I have heard about 'em" (about Will-o'-the-Wisps, that is), "and the fairies too, from your grandfather and grandmother!"

But not then, nor ever afterwards, could he be persuaded to tell any of those tales. It is conceivable that the whole subject seemed wicked to his devoutly religious mind.

Chapter 16 *Mr. Smith's Chatter*

MUCH, though by no means all, that I have told about old Farnborough was gathered in talk with John Smith in the cottage after he had left his farm. Sometimes he spoke of old acquaintances; sometimes of obsolete customs. His well-stored memory, turned over and over, has left me with an impression of whimsical good-temper, of sober and quiet laughter, slightly boyish in the love of oddity, yet always well poised like a self-possessed man's. My uncle had experienced the taste of life and squared it with his religious convictions. He knew too much, and he was too kindly, to be anything but tolerant. Sorrow, of which he had had his share, had not soured him; of hourly aches and pains he had taken the measure; death and change came into the scheme of things he held it a duty to think about at bed-time and on Sundays. He could afford to be amused at life; for at the back of it he was conversant with and revered its greatness. After his death a curate he had liked well related how the rector of the parish once advised, as a sovereign remedy against down-heartedness, going to have a chat with Mr. John Smith. And I think that fairly stamps his quality. You needed not

A Farmer's Life

cease being serious with him, yet you might all the time see the comical side of things.

I'll own that sometimes he was tedious, prosy. Platitudes which others eschewed had for him the savour of profound truths. He almost wallowed in any little technicalities of law that came his way. For ceremony, especially for church ceremony, he had a tiresome appetite. When a new church was consecrated—he had been active on the committee—he was proud to walk as churchwarden in front of the bishop; for he, if no one else, felt the solemnity of the occasion. Sincerely he was testifying to his faith—his grey head helped, his hobbling walk. He could show what an old man thought of such things. His shrewdness, not small, was kept for worldly matters: in church, bishop or none, it behoved him to make a show of reverence.

Those who knew him best knew this side of his character and were careful never to distress him with any sign of flippancy. And this was noticeable: tolerant though he was to others, as I have said, he was never tolerant towards himself. And, without exacting it, he looked for nothing else than decorum in deed and thought from all who were truly dear to him. One had to be careful, therefore, not to shock him. Yet he judged outsiders by no such high standard. Their slips tickled him. And, being a great

Mr. Smith's Chatter

tease, he rather liked hearing of behaviour in others—irritating, " aggravating " behaviour—such as he never would have condescended to himself. At the same time it pleased him to be rather provoking. On his farm more than once he caused some tree or other to be cut down before he asked permission ; and if any of his family protested that the landlord might not be pleased, his rejoinder was to urge " He can't make me put it up again, can he ? " And this was characteristic. As he behaved to his landlord so he loved to see others behave in other things. It was his delight to see personality asserting itself—pushing itself close up against circumstance or against other personality. Obstinacy—that, to tell the truth, was fully developed in him. Only, he was at heart so kind a man that, instead of being seriously annoying, his obstinacy was only laughable.

Few men can have been less ostentatious than he was. He never tried to " shine " ; was as well content to listen as to talk. And if he sometimes exclaimed against himself for being " such a talkative old man," he had provocation enough to excuse talking. He must have known that we enjoyed hearing him, as indeed we did ; for not the long-forgotten scent of new bread that used to pervade the Farnborough farm-house in our childhood was more agreeable than his

123

A Farmer's Life

" old tales "—so suggestive of country doings. So he talked—even a little unwillingly at times ; yet oftener as if he couldn't help it, whenever some remark could be illustrated by a telling anecdote from his own long experience.

Such an anecdote—how was it called up, I wonder ?—related to old Mr. Calloway, who long ago had befriended his (John Smith's) father as a young man. Mr. Calloway employed a man who disliked being hurried. Being urged to " Get on, Jack ; get that finished," Jack answered, " What's the good, master ? You knows very well as soon as I get this job done you got another looked out for me."

Human affairs went on for Mr. Smith at a deeper level, I mean with a closer touch on daily life, than is reached by political theory ; and that was well for me, for in politics we only agreed in differing. The Licensing Bill of 1908 found us quite at odds. But our discussions of it brought back to my uncle's memory just the sort of anecdote—perverse, deplorable, yet with more than a touch of the comic—which pleased him to tell.

In his young days, he said, public-houses were open all night, or at any rate they were hardly closed before it was time to reopen. Then he recalled a certain " old Tom, a bad old chap," who took advantage of this circumstance.

Mr. Smith's Chatter

In Farnborough at that time there were three licensed houses—the "Ship," the "Tumbledown Dick," and Bridger's. Bridger's, my uncle remarked, as if it was the most ordinary thing in the world, Bridger's was "a Tom and Jerry."

"What's a 'Tom and Jerry'?" I exclaimed —as I was no doubt expected to do.

"I was just goin' to tell you if you'd give me time," my uncle said, sarcastically. Then he explained. A "Tom and Jerry" was a shop where you could buy groceries, and also beer, doubtless to be drunk on the premises.

Of the three licensed houses in Farnborough old Tom was a constant patron, troubled, however, by his wife trying to get him home. It would happen in this way. She would find him drinking at Bridger's and bid him to come home. "All right," he would answer meekly: "let's just finish this little I got here," and he would offer her a sip from his mug. So she was induced to sit down and make herself comfortable.

Then, before the mug was empty, he would say, in a deprecating manner, "I must jest go outside a minute," and so would go out, leaving her expectant of his return.

But, instead of returning, he made his way to the "Ship," where he could have a nicish time before his wife at last found him. At the "Ship," on some different plea, the woman was once more left waiting for him to come back, while he was in fact making his way to the " Tumbledown Dick."

Eventually from the "Tumbledown Dick" too he was hunted out; slipping away, getting the start, and presently reaching Bridger's again. But not now to be disturbed. Once there for the second time he was secure for the remainder of the evening, the wife not caring to begin the hunt all over again.

It may very well be that this was not quite the sort of story that was found so effective for cheering up a despondent curate. Mr. Smith had a great fund of anecdotes, and would have been unlikely to offend sensitive ears by telling anything liable to distress them. On the other hand, one never knew beforehand—himself as little as anybody—what he was going to recall next. Well-told anecdotes were, in fact, not the staple of his talk. They came from him, and in abundance—often with a little bursting laugh—as the seasoning to something else; but the true quality was something quite different—something better worth remembering, if only memory could recover it at all: an easy-going conversation; a very sane and tranquil comment on current events. It was always good-tempered. A touch of Hampshire dialect flavoured it; through and through it seemed expressive of a mellow country

wisdom and an Old English faith. Certainly
it is not to be supposed that John Smith had ever
even glanced at any doctrines other than those of
the Church of England; but apart from this I
think he always felt, though he never spoke of,
a certain dignity in the collective life of the
English. Their doings, especially in country
places, fascinated him more than he knew. He
had been in touch with so much that was going on;
and it had been going on so long, and so valiantly,
and on the whole with so much efficiency, that he
was always optimistic, full of reverence, full of
kindly laughter. His talk gave that impression
—I wish I could give a sample of it. Anecdotes
bubbled out of him oftener than he knew; but
always, at back of them, could be felt the serene
English poise of a wise outlook.

One sample of the talk—not in itself a very
good one—alone remains, the sentences scribbled
down while they were still hot in my memory.
And it is but the words that are left: the tone of
them, the geniality, cannot be recovered. Even
the scene is hard to restore. It was in the cow-
stalls one winter evening. By lantern light Mr.
Smith was milking, with one of his sons near by.
Outside one may imagine the vast winter night.
Within the cow-stall I stood, enjoying the little
core of light and the warmth of the animals,
hearing their quiet breathing and chewing, the

occasional rattle of their chains. Mr. Smith sat with his head butted into the flank of a cow. The son came to the light, emptying new milk into a larger pail; then said:

" I hear they been rough-musickin' young Fred Stoner." (He named, not by that name indeed, an employer of the neighbourhood.)

Mr. Smith raised his head from the cow's flank to say, " Eh ? " And his son repeated, " I hear they been rough-musickin' young Fred Stoner."

" Oh ? When was that ? "

" Laſt night and the night before. They went all round his house the firſt night; but laſt night I underſtand he had the police there. I don't know whether they copped the ringleader or no."

" What was it for, d'ye know ? "

" No. I didn't hear. . . . "

" Ah, well, we shall hear. It'll all come out in time. But it shows a man ain't very popular, don't it ? "

Discussion of Mr. Stoner's deserts followed, and of the possibility of his having " come out " to meet the mob. His deserts were not rated high. As to the possibility, Mr. Smith, pushing back his ſtool (for the milking was done), said:

" I don't suppose he'd face 'em. But 'tain't much of fun, if he don't come out to 'em."

Mr. Smith's Chatter

The son said, " I went to a rough-musicking
once. 'Tain't half bad fun, I can tell you. . .
When they rough-musicked old Jim Bones."

" Ah, old Jim Bones. You knowed him,
didn't you ? " Mr. Smith addressed me. And
since I couldn't remember Mr. Bones, he explained : " He wa'n't much of a lot. He was
Mrs. So-and-so's father-in-law. . . . Not that
that makes him any the better—nor she any the
worse, if it comes to that."

I assented. " That's the sort of thing nobody
can help. But what did they rough-music him
for ? "

" Why, 'twas like this. He lived in one of
a pair of cottages up at ——, you know. And in
the other was his sister's husband, that had married
again. They never took to his second wife—
never got on together. And as soon as the old
man died, Jim Bones or some of his household
was in there, moving things out and taking 'em
away, before even he was buried. They began
to pull the house to pieces while he lay there in
his coffin."

" I see. And so the people rough-musicked
him. Serve him right. Did he come out to 'em ? "

The son said, " No. He never came out.
Still, 'twa'n't half bad fun, for all that."

But his father commented, " Ah, they ought
to come out. Not like old Hole did, though."

I

A Farmer's Life

" Hole ? "

" Yes, the butcher. He came out to 'em, and he never went in again. He fell down dead on the doorstep."

" Apoplexy ? "

" Yes; and his getting into such a temper, don't you see." Mr. Smith rose to his tottering feet, preparing to hang up the milking stool, and added, with a little explosion of laughter, " But the best of it was, that 'twasn't for him they were rough-musicking at all. 'Twas his foreman. But he took the matter up; and he *was* in a passion, by all accounts ! There, poor old feller, it killed him."

Chapter 17 *More Chatter*

THE flavour of Mr. Smith's talk was never much affected by his infirmities. He was as it were a voice sounding invariably of English country or country folk— of fields and labour, of villagers and village interests. He had what might be called a folk mind. So much was this the case that sometimes it was impossible to determine whether a whimsical idea of his own was being told, or a piece of genuine traditional lore.

Which was it, for example—I think it must have been his own invention—that inspired that teasing pleasing theory of his about walnut trees? He assured me, with all the air of village conviction, that when a walnut tree died the man who planted it would also die within the year. Be it noted, this was apropos of a walnut tree I wanted to move in my own garden, planted by myself some years previously. But Mr. Smith gave several examples to prove his assertion. He seemed to have had a fairly large experience of walnut trees and their owners.

Almost certainly of true folk origin was his tale of a doctor, which he fathered, in quite the customary way, upon a local practitioner he named and had known long ago. The tale went that this doctor was making up pills with pestle and mortar, while his man—who couldn't read but was to deliver the pills—waited and watched. At last they were put into their boxes and handed to the man, whereupon he began straightway to name the patients they were for. "This box," he said, "is for Lady Gray at the Grange; and this other for old Dame Russell at the workhouse."

The doctor stared. "That's all right," he said, "but how the devil did you know?"

"Why," the man explained, "when you was making up Lady Gray's I heard the pestle saying in the mortar, 'Linger along, linger along.' But presently it begun to say, 'Die and be damned, die and be damned,' and then I knew 'twas for poor old Mother Russell."

Mr. Smith's comment on a case of shingles reported to him was no jocular folk-tale like this last, but a sober expression of village belief, old as the hills and noteworthy for a queer twist-up of ideas in it. Is not "strength" in health, or in iron, or in the staff of life, or in intoxicants, always the same sort of thing? Identity of name proves it: English rustics had acted on the belief for centuries. My uncle spoke as if he himself thought there was something in it.

For, at the mention of shingles, "nasty weakening disease," he said, "In the old times, if you had shingles you went to the blacksmith."

More Chatter

" The blacksmith ? "

" Yes, to get him to put a little wheat into his iron ladle and melt the oil out of it." Any oil is good, Mr. Smith opined, but the oil from wheat, he supposed, had a special virtue. " Wheat, you see, is the strongest thing we know," and is therefore everybody's food. " If you get a barrel of old ale and put some wheat in it to steep, then you must look out for trouble."

" Why ? "

" Because you can't carry it." In other words, old ale, " strengthened " by the strength of wheat, is an intoxicant too strong for ordinary men.

To " take up your back day " was a phrase my uncle used for dying. He explained it as a common alternative metaphor for " getting the sack " ; and it originated, he said, in the custom of paying a man on Saturday up to Friday evening only, so that there remains a day still to be paid for. During harvesting or haying, this secures that a man will come back to work next week, instead of straying off to another job. But of course, if he means leaving, he can " take up his back day."

So far Mr. Smith. Yet an old-fashioned flavour in his talk may have come from a more ancient origin than he knew. In old Manorial Court Rolls a tenant was often said to have

133

" closed his last day " when he died. It is not unlikely that the phrase my uncle attributed to present-day industrial customs had in fact been wandering to and fro across the country for centuries.

Now and again details about farm-work were mentioned in the course of his talk. A truss of hay, he said, should weigh fifty-six lbs., or, of " new hay," sixty lbs. The hay is " new " if it is cut out before the next October following the hay-making. After that it is " old." My uncle had known a hay-tier who could cut out and " tie " as many as seventy trusses in a day, with a boy to help him twisting the bands.

Again, with more antiquated suggestiveness (for the implement was all but obsolete already) he spoke of a flail and named its parts. The " handstaff " led off, followed by the " start "— an iron knob or button in the upper end of the handstaff. Next was the " capping "—a piece of bent wood turned over the end of the handstaff with a slot in it to receive a leather connection fixed on to the start. This leather strap was called the " middle band." Finally, hanging to the leather, was the loose-swinging staff, called the " swingel," that word being pronounced with a soft g, as in angel. To hear these old words was to be carried back in fancy to the barn at Farnborough, where they must have been familiar enough to John Smith while he was still

More Chatter

a little boy. A long-forgotten fragrance seemed to cling to them—a lost quiet.

But this fragrance, this quiet, proceeded probably from the old man's quiet mind whatever he spoke of, and made it singularly pleasant to be with him—to stroll with him hobbling up and down the garden behind his cottage, or into the little wood of birches at the side. At the far end of the garden he had a fowl-run, and near it a shed where he stabled the pony for his milk-round. And in the garden, along with potatoes and cabbages for his own use (but he had a few roses and pansies too), to say nothing of the rhubarb which he showed me how to grow ("Take it up and leave it kickin' about all the winter," he laughed, as if the manure from the pony's stable had nothing to do with it)—in the garden he used to grow mangold for the pony—to grow and harvest the crop in the same manner as he would have done a larger crop on his farm.

Separated from the garden by a ditch and a low bank was the little wood of birch trees already mentioned, tangled with thickets of brambles and a few scrubby oaks. Through this maze my uncle once led me to a disused gravel-pit half full of water, as was only to be expected in that waterlogged soil. The place was pretty enough, with its banks, fern-edged, overhanging the water, dark amongst the trees ; but what Mr. Smith especially wished me to see was a brood of

A Farmer's Life

young moor-chicks that had been hatched and were swimming about in that secluded spot. His delight in them illustrated a side of his character yet to be noticed.

He was indeed no naturalist. Darwin's theories, if he ever heard of them, had left no mark on his orthodox faith. The only sign he ever gave of a suspicion that men and apes might be somehow related was a strong dislike, almost a horror, he harboured for monkeys in any shape or form. This dislike he carried so far as to disapprove of " Monkey-brand " soap because of the advertisements of that useful commodity. From something he once said I conceived the idea that monkeys were revolting to his sense of man's worth—they were too painfully human. However that may be, in this one objection he sufficiently exhibited a prejudice that would have armed him against modern natural history. But this did not prevent his indulgence of a sort of eighteenth-century enjoyment of " nature." Theories he neither knew nor cared for. On the other hand, he was as interested as a boy in the bird life and animal life to be seen about his fields, in the course of his daily work.

How pleased he was (more than once he told of it in my hearing) to recall his holding up of a neighbour on the road one day. " Don't ye see the road's stopped ? " he had exclaimed, and had pointed to a weasel that was convoying a litter

More Chatter

of young ones across the road, and was standing to show fight to the intruding men. John Smith spoke with admiration, not at all as if he regarded weasels as enemies.

He told me that, for some years before he gave up, hares had disappeared from his farm, because, he thought, coursing had been abandoned. No longer hunted, the hares had resumed their habit of following definite " runs," and had been too easy a prey for poachers. So Mr. Smith argued.

One summer afternoon, being then a very old man, he sat in my garden watching, with excited exclamations of delight, the coming and going of a " bee-bird " as he called it—a fly-catcher. " There he goes," he said, time after time, as the little bird swooped from its chosen stand on a low branch. Nothing then would satisfy Mr. Smith until he had determined where the nest must be ; and after that his account of the large broods hatched by fly-catchers showed that he must have been an active birds'-nester in his boyhood. Another thing that interested him that afternoon was the visit of a small flock of tits, that hovered and fluttered over a water-pan set under an old apple tree. " What a lot of 'em ! " I murmured. " All one brood, no doubt," my uncle said.

It felt good to be there. With the apple trees, and the birds, and the May-time, the old farmer's mind seemed much in tune.

137

Chapter 18 *Ebbing Powers*

ONE of the most affecting things about John Smith's advancing age was the habit he fell into—few noticed it, and himself perhaps least of all—of letting a faint sound of despondency escape him now and then. After a brief liveliness it would come—as if he had thought of something further to say, then felt it to be vanity after all—a sigh, an expression of tedium, a " hm, hm," in descending scale, no sooner uttered than suppressed. He talked, laughed, as of old; relapsed, as of old, into silence and then, presently, almost unnoticed, came the faint " hm, hm, hm," as of a disillusioned man.

What did it mean ? Was the pain he suffered racking him again ? That was the first hypothesis. He was in almost constant pain. Acute rheumatism—if it was not neuritis—took him across the hips and seldom left him. What more likely than that a twinge too hard to bear was drawing from him an involuntary and scarce-veiled groan ? That's just how he would have met cruel pain—momentarily allowing his feelings some outlet, and then checking himself for fear of distressing those he loved.

Yet probably this was not the whole, if it was

Ebbing Powers

a part, of the explanation. More likely he was troubled in another way—as a man clinging hopelessly to the edge of a cliff would be troubled, feeling his grasp weakening, his fingers giving way one after the other. The cliff of which John Smith was gradually losing grip was Life. Not that he feared Death. But the touch of circumstance in all his faculties had been very intimate, and he was loth to lose it. Even troublesome things had made their call to his vigour; and now that he had to turn his back on the very troubles, and the calls even from them had to be disregarded, it was rubbed into him from every side that his vigour was waning, that the messages from the outer world would never quicken his faculties again.

It may be assumed that he felt this keenly when he retired from the farm. In putting off the cares of business he was also putting off the stimulus they could give. He was letting go life with one hand. And daily, hourly, there would be some reminder, taunting him for having turned away. Did he now avoid muddying his boots in the farm-yard? It was a proof that he was no longer a strong man. Was he unable any longer to go to Blackwater Fair? Why, of course, his time was over. He, who had been wont to do everything for himself, now had to have everything done for him; and the

139

A Farmer's Life

devoted affection that surrounded him, never-failing, was still not the same thing as the touches of struggle which had once assured him of strength. After all, his joy had been less in getting things done than in the doing of them; and that was all past for him. It is no wonder if he sometimes sighed audibly. The zest of life was departing. It was crumbling away from his grasp. Daily he was losing hold.

The progress of this change was as slow as it was sure. There was plenty of time for him to feel every hopeless pang—to watch his world escaping him inch by inch. Long after he could no longer get down to milk a cow he was able to go through Farnborough village with his milk; long after he lost the strength to deliver the milk himself he could travel with a grandson and so pass the time of day with his old cronies. Yet he might not totter to the back-doors and taste the village intimacies; he had to keep to the high-road, nor see over the hedges; and only so in the better weather. It was like looking on at his own slow dissolution.

But at least it was slow. He was still able to walk, that day he came to my house to see his last living sister, Ann, then on her death-bed. On the following Sunday afternoon, when I went to him to tell of her death, he had come down-stairs, and saw me from his window, where he

140

Ebbing Powers

sat looking at the summer weather and at the aeroplanes from the Farnborough factory circling in the sky. Over those fields he had once seen Will-o'-the-Wisp, and now . . . Now his last sister was dead—he divined it as soon as he saw me. Of the old family none was left save himself alone; yet he could still creep about. He had the use of his feet for Ann's funeral; and once afterwards, for a family gathering to settle up her small affairs. But this was almost the last time. Soon he took to a bath-chair, in which, a helpless cripple, he continued to see the more public roads of the neighbourhood. Once that neighbourhood had entered into his life so keenly, with the challenge of contact on all sides. He had loved the touch. But it was hardly to be got from a bath-chair more than it would have been from a motor-car. What he felt I do not know. He seemed cheerful; chatted as of old; gave no other sign of being bored. Only, now and then, it was hard to resist the impression that he was feeling tired of life, when one heard from him that unintended and half-unconscious sigh.

Chapter 19 A Rally

1 : *Mr. Smith's Manner*

I DO not know in what spirits my uncle got through the winter that followed his sister's death. An outdoor man like he was may feel it a reminder of his infirmities to be obliged to sit all day by the fire. But with the return of summer he recovered for a little while —no, not the use of his limbs, but full enjoyment at least of his older memories.

You see, he was now, for the first time in his life, a gentleman of leisure and could get away from home for more than a day; for he had no cows to feed and milk. Certainly, once before he had gone for a few days' holiday to Horsham —I cannot imagine when or how. Apart from that he had had no outings longer than ten or twelve hours, in all the years I had known him. It is not to be supposed that he felt this a grievance. Countrymen of his sort find their way so lovingly into the details, the inner charms, of their neighbourhood that they cannot understand why others ever want to go away.

But at last my uncle, unable any longer to taste the joys familiar to him, and reduced to more common delights, was not at all unwilling

A Rally

to leave home for a change. So, in the summer of 1914 (it was June, to be precise) he was persuaded to spend a few days—nearly a week in all—in my house.

I cannot remember how he managed the journey. Did he sit in his bath-chair in the guard's van? At any rate he came here from the railway station in his bath-chair, his daughter watching over him like an anxious mother over a sick child; and within limits he was as pleased as a careless visitor to the seaside. The limits, to be sure, were narrow. He could not move from one chair to another without help. Sometimes pain in his thighs drew groans from him and he was near to fainting. To get upstairs—his bedroom had to be upstairs—he was obliged to go sitting up one step at a time, with somebody at the landing to lift him finally into the chair put for him there; and in some such way, I believe, he got down again o' mornings, after I had gone to my work. This sort of thing severely limited his enjoyment. Much of the garden he had liked of old was out of his reach on any terms.

On the other hand, his bath-chair gave him opportunities almost new to him. It furnished a comfortable seat in shady places he had never thought of until now, when he could be wheeled to them and could rest for hours. Better still,

A Farmer's Life

it enabled us to take him, along by-paths (for
motor-cars were a nuisance on the roads), into
parts as unlike his own level fields as need be;
and he looked almost with wonder at the valley
and the gullies and the shaggy heaths of the
Bourne. Had he but been forty years old
instead of over eighty! The interest of thrusting
one's faculties into a new neighbourhood quick-
ened in him even as it was.

And, thanks perhaps to this recovery of spirits,
his memories of older times grew richer. This
was our evening programme—from a short
outing we would get back home to a fairly early
supper, and then, after lighting a lamp, would
sit chatting until bed-time by the table, from
which it was difficult for him to move. All his
former life, and especially the earlier years,
seemed to come back to him with revived interest,
if not with delight. Many of the details worked
into the narrative of his father were obtained in
those evenings; and then too it was that I got
some particulars of his own childhood, as now
set down in the earlier chapters of this book.
Farnborough village, Welsh cattle, the " Tumbledown Dick," Dog-traction, Jack the Matchman,
Machinery Riots, and so on, drifted in vivid
pictures across his memory. Most of it was not
new to me, or did but add a point or two to
what was already known. Yet I was very

144

willing to listen. It was like a reading in George Borrow, only far more vivid, more intimate, more homely. Above all, it betrayed none of the acrimony that is to be found in Borrow, none of the dissatisfaction. For example, in the *Romany Rye* the roads all seem dusty, the country folk for the most part hard, mean, selfish. But, in my uncle's memories, early Victorian England was a happy place on the whole, even if now and then, as though from a great distance, came sounds of hardship and struggle. The people appeared to mean well and to enjoy life; and the country things were pleasant to think about —pleasant as old china—when recalled in John Smith's quiet tones.

It occurred to me once that he was one of the very few men I had known who could be truly said to have made a success of the art of living. He had achieved it not consciously or intentionally so much as by adhering to the old-fashioned rural traditions of good behaviour; being patient, cheerful, neighbourly, and keeping close in touch with natural things. Few, nowadays, know rural life as he knew it. He was indeed no peasant, though almost poor enough; but a century earlier he would have been a yeoman. The country—its materials, soil, weather, animals, people—with all these he had worked; not as a stranger, not as an aloof

K

A Farmer's Life

exploiter or patronising admirer, but as a comrade and an expert. That was the impression he still gave. He was no gentleman-resident or tourist, but a strong and confident provincial. His cheerfulness was a symptom of his success. One evening, I own, he broke into sobbing. It came from an emotion largely of thankfulness for the happiness he was feeling. But as a rule he was in good heart, if never exactly jolly.

His manner of talk was worth watching—very quiet and easy ; now and then hanging up for a word or for a name, now and then gathering into a little rush on top of a gentle splash of laughter. Then there were minutes—not dragged out, yet making appreciable pauses—in which he seemed to be collecting strength to go on again, or to be forcing himself, perhaps, to take no notice of the pain in his limbs. His eyes looked tired ; he shut them for a moment or so in exhaustion. His lips too he put together with a patient air. Then, the lips parting, there was an instant's indrawing of breath before speech began again —an indrawing, a momentary hesitation, as if to make quite sure that nobody else wanted to speak. He would not intrude his memories ; he would not interrupt. If you had something to say, his manner seemed to urge that your talk would be more important than his. Only, in the event of your not wishing to make any remark

A Rally

—why, there were such and such memories turning over and over in his mind, which he was not disinclined to tell.

A very quiet and contemplative " making remarks," with pauses of circumspection, reverie —that is what it amounted to, hardly giving an impression of being continuous talk. I sat listening, fascinated—listening as it were to memories rather than to uttered words, feeling as if I myself had seen the coaches, taken the waggon to the Farnham clay-pits, hobnobbed with old Mr. Callaway, or what not. Until my uncle wanted to go to bed I listened. I helped get him upstairs, and afterwards went to him in bed to wish him good-night; and then I sat late to hurry down on paper memoranda of the evening and of some (by no means all) of the things I had been hearing.

Chapter 20 *A Rally*

2 : *Conversation*

MUCH of the talk referred to old people, long forgotten. One fragment alone of this kind seemed worth saving. It told of a certain rich man (named to me) who in his old age married a young wife. She, at any rate, whether he liked it or not, developed a taste for gaiety, and entertained parties. And at these parties the old husband sometimes fell asleep, nor could be disturbed whatever might be going on—singing or what you will. But then, he was apt to awake suddenly; and in that case he would start immediately upon some song of his own and sing it to the end, regardless of the guests or of anything he might have interrupted.

This seems to have been told on the first day of my uncle's visit. The following night he went to bed with diminished pain, but almost over-filled with emotion. It was Sunday; and after supper, while I sat with him at the table, his daughter and the rest of the family went into the next room and began singing hymns. They chose old-fashioned favourites, of his mother's period, ending with " Rock of Ages."

A Rally

As I sat by the old man—both of us very quiet—a perception of his great appreciation touched me keenly. I could discern the value to him, and to others in his plight, of that old faith in a future life which these hymns were celebrating. An emotion went prickling through me. This man beside me, old and worn-out, in almost constant pain, with no hope in this world, and wondering (I am sure he had been wondering that day) if he would ever see another summer—this man was finding refreshment, and contentment, in the promise the hymns repeated. It was almost startling. I was smitten with admiration to see how well they fitted his case.

In an interval he murmured, " I haven't had such a treat for a long time." In another interval he asked me, since he could not go himself, to peep into the next room, to see if his daughter " looked as if she was enjoyin' herself," as though he would wager she was and no mistake.

Then he told me a notable thing. " I had a visit," he murmured, " a week or two ago from a woman who was servant when —— was ill." He named his wife, who had died of a cancer long ago. " I was glad to see her " (the sometime servant). " I dessay for two years, while —— was so bad, this girl 'd get up any time o' night and spend half the night singing to her. . . . Well, —— knew I couldn't sing ; and the girl, she perhaps 'd hear, and get up and come along and sit singin'—half the night."

No doubt it was hymns that the girl sang. But anyhow, " I've always thought highly of her ever since," John Smith said.

After he had got into bed and wished me " Good-night; God bless you," — words he uttered with deep fervour,—he gave a sort of sob and added, " I'm so thankful that we've been spared, the two of us, for this. And it's doin' —— so much good." He named his daughter.

The next night a little earthen basin—a penny thing I had brought from Caudebec—was put on the table for cigarette ashes. My uncle fingered it appreciatively, but wondered how it could have been taken off the potter's wheel; for it had no flat bottom, like the flower-pots he was used to, but stood on a raised rim. It was puzzling to know how that could have been done. Leaving that, however, Mr. Smith surmised that the potter must have had a delicate " ribber," and, after several technical explanations, remarked, " Now I'm got so old I feel ashamed I didn't learn more " about the potting. His father put him to it; but he told his father, " I'll learn any other trade you put me to, but if I'm set to the potting I'll never follow it."

A Rally

" Then 'ten't no use to teach ye," was the answer, or the gist of it.

I gathered that in his boyhood John Smith had a positive distaste for his father's trade. He " didn't like the smell of it. . . . There was an earthy smell, and a leady smell." Perhaps also the lead disturbed him in another way. At any rate I heard once more how his father's hands were twisted up and useless as a result of the use of the lead, and—although this could not have affected his decision at that early date—he now surmised that lead poisoning had undermined the health both of his father and brother and brought about their death long before they were as full of years as himself. Still, in spite of his dislike, he did learn a little of the trade, and was able to " set a square "—that is, to place the pots in the proper order, according to trade requirements for counting and pricing.

There followed many details about the Farnborough pottery—I think they have all been gathered into the earlier volume (*William Smith*); and this too: " You never see now any of that Staffordshire yellow ware," all " streaked " and " ornamented with roses." And since this had of old been brought into Farnborough in little low coster-carts drawn by dogs, it naturally led to talk about dog-traction, whence we branched off to many other matters.

151

A Farmer's Life

After telling of the owls whose nests he used to rob in " the old pollard " at Farnborough, he strayed into talk about animal life in general. Of owls themselves first. He had learnt their value. " Anybody as kills one ought to have a month for it." For they prey on the little " vowls " (rhyme to " fowls ") that do so much harm in grass land, gnawing just under the roots. For weasels and stoats also he entertained a real respect. He would not have them destroyed; nor yet even hedgehogs. For the last-named, it is true, he had to confess some dislike: in a pasture with cows he felt hedgehogs out of place. But he owned that he had no evidence against them, and was probably biassed by old country tales.

Once more he spoke of the pluck of weasels, as I have already told, and he also remarked on the horrible stench weasels throw out when hard pressed. Then he discoursed of partridges and their large broods—eighteen or twenty in a covey; and of hares. One hare, while he was still at the farm, a man had shot and given to him, " because she was too big to carry away " secretly. For this man was " no sportsman "; he had " smooched " the hare. My uncle, paunching it, had found within two families. There were leverets just ready for birth; and there were others, much younger. " The

A Rally

ſtrangeſt animal I know," he commented, with
a touch of awe as if speaking of something
uncanny. He had heard of hares keeping two
families going at once—perhaps five miles apart;
but this he had not aċtually known at firſt hand.
Only he reasoned that diſtance did not matter
much, to a hare.

To him, inseċt life seemed " more wonderful "
than the life of larger things. " The little
bits of things—gnats, cheese-mites—— And
yet, when you look at it, it's alive ! " It puzzled
him what use they could be; for they were all
" sent " for our use. But, in this conneċtion,
what was to be thought of emmets ? He " never
could see the use of emmets," unless, he laughed,
for their eggs, to feed pheasants.

Of the much that followed—of pigs and old
Farnborough; of his father; of Welsh cattle
and sheep; of various squires—I think there is
nothing left to be told. Only there was one old
workman, spoken of as " Old Tom," whose
surname may as well be suppressed, of whom a
few particulars were new to me.

This old chap took a literally singular pride in
having been the laſt man to be put in the ſtocks
at Farnborough. One Sunday he went to sleep
in church, and snored loudly. " The sexton
came along with his cane and gave him a
ſtripe. . . . Waked him up, and ' Damn it ! ' he

153

A Farmer's Life

hollered, ' what be ye got up to now ? ' So then they hauled 'n out o' church and put 'n in the stocks for brawlin' in church."

This man was once cutting hedges for my uncle. " It used to be a perquisite of the man that was cuttin' a hedge to take home any of the dead wood in a nitch. None of the other he wasn't entitled to, but only the dead. Old Tom was goin' home with a biggish nitch, when Hughes met 'n. Hughes was bailiff at Farnborough Park. ' What ye got there ? ' he says. ' Why, hedge-cuttin's,' old Tom says. ' D'your master know what you be at ? ' Hughes says. ' What business is that of yours ? ' old Tom says. ' Well,' Hughes says, ' I knows if 'twas my old man he'd very soon have ye for it.' ' Yes,' Tom says ; ' but I en't workin' for your old man. I be workin' for Mister Smith.'

" One day after that he was a bit drunk and rolled into a ditch—there used to be a open ditch down there by the bridge. Hughes happened to come along, and pulled 'n out and set 'n in the bank across t'other side of the road—and he set there and sweared at 'n for it. But Hughes went on down to the ' Prince o' Wales ' —told 'm what had happened and that old Tom was there, and said he'd give 'em five shillin's to fetch a cab so that he could take 'n home. But when he got back to the bridge with the cab, there was old Tom in the ditch again. He'd crawled back. ' Damn it,' he said, ' I'd sooner bide there an' drown than I'd take a favour from that man ! " *

I don't think Mr. Smith realised that he had been repeating a folk-tale. He had probably heard it in juſt the same way himself, and it seemed fairly illuſtrative of old Tom's charaċter. He went on :

" Did I ever tell ye how your aunt Susan county-courted him ? She was a very extravagant woman, his wife was. . . . And of course, where a man couldn't keep a regular job there was a good deal o' loſt time. . . . One time he aſt me if I couldn't give 'n a job o' work. Yes, I says ; he could split some wood your aunt Susan wanted for her bread oven. . . . So after he'd bin at it about two hours his two daughters come down to the shop with a written order for some bread, and loaf-sugar, and gammon of bacon. Plums and currants I think there was too. . . . So Susan come out to me with the paper. ' Have ye got old Tom at work for ye, then ? ' she says. ' Yes,' I says, ' he bin here a little while.' ' Well, look at this.' ' That's pretty good,' I says, ' when he en't earnt nothin' yet.' So she went back an' told the gals they could have some bread and some loaf-sugar, but

* Note C, Appendix.

they'd have to do without the raisins and currants, and she shouldn't cut a gammon for 'em —'cause they wanted the middle cut.

" He kep' on work and got a little wood split. And in the evenin' I had to pass by where he was workin' and he says, ' Master, I wants to speak to ye.'

" ' Well, what is it, Tom ? ' I says.

" ' I wants to ast ye somethin'. Do you think God Almighty ever made a man to work all day without any vittles or drink in him ? '

" ' Well, Tom,' I says, ' God A'mighty have made all sorts of queer things ; and He've made one man so contrairy as *he*'ll do it.' . . . I've often laughed about it since. . . . But that was the trouble with old Tom. He ,was so contrairy. He always stood in his own light.

" Called to me one day, he did : ' Mister Smith, I wants to speak to ye. . . . I wants to ast ye a question. Will ye give me your advice ? '

" ' I dunno as it's much good,' I says ; ' but I ain't heard what it is.'

" ' Why,' he says, ' Higgins have jest bought this farm down here and wants somebody to look after it, and his son have recommended me for the job. D'you think I better take it ? '

" ' Well,' I says, ' he couldn't do better. You could do the work all right. But since you've asked my opinion I'll give it to ye. I knows

156

what sort of man you be; and I knows what sort of man Higgins is; and I don't think you'll be there a fortnight without quarrellin'.' 'Damn it!' he says, 'I won't go near the place!' And he never did."

My uncle had forgotten about the county-court process. He continued, telling still of old Tom:

"Dug a field for me, he did—him and his two sons. And when 'twas over they measured 'n, and then I sent for a practical man—but I'm before my story. Will had just got a new land chain, and he measured it, and made it come to about four rod more. 'Well,' I said, 'bothered if I'll take old Tom's measure!' So then ('twas a bit of contrairiousness on my part) I sent to 'em and says, 'If we can get the right measure I'll square up with ye.' So they got a practical man—one of these as went about doin' that sort of thing—and he made it come to less. . . . Yes, less than their measure. 'Twasn't but a shillin' or so. . . . Well, old Tom come to square up, and I says to 'n, 'Look here, you owes me about a shillin'. You've drawed more 'n it comes to. But I won't ask ye for that,' I says, 'if you'll take the measure your man have made.' 'Well,' old Tom says, 'you've grubbed out the hedges and cleaned out them that's left, and the field comes to less than he used to be.

A Farmer's Life

I should ha' thought what you've done would ha' made 'n bigger.' "

One other scrap of this talk is worth recalling. The subject was hay-making, as to which my uncle admitted that the old methods did produce on the whole a better quality of hay than the newer methods. But, he urged, where a farmer would send a foreman and twenty women in the old times, now he could get a carter, and a pony in a machine, to do more in a few hours than of old the gang would do in a day. And doing it in the old way, with hay at its present price (that is, the price at the time of this talk), you would be losing money.

Of rick-firing there was a good deal of technical talk, and of the way to cut a rick out in such a case—getting ladders and hay-cutting knives, to work down into the centre. The cut-out stuff being spread on the ground was liable to burst into flame if the wind caught it. Once (but only once) my uncle had seen a waggon going along the road with hay in such a state that little wisps falling off here and there began to flare up on the road.

Many years ago—in the old Farnborough days—he had finished building a rick near the farm-house. The next morning two sons of Mr. Longman, his landlord—two lads at that time—came to him, presumably sent by their

158

A Rally

father from the big house at Farnborough Hill about half a mile away. They brought an urgent message that there was some hay going wrong somewhere. Probably their father had smelt it in the night. At any rate something was wrong, somewhere; they could assure Mr. Smith of that, although they couldn't say where.

" Come along with me," said Mr. Smith, " and I'll show you the rick."

" Why ! " they exclaimed, " however did you know where it is ? "

" If you was to make one yourselves," Mr. Smith answered, " and try to sleep afterwards, you'd very soon find out how anybody knows."

Chapter 21 *Collapse*

MY uncle's visit in June had been so successful he did not need any urging to repeat it, and in October he came again, bath-chair and all. But the four months had made a difference. It would not have been, in any case, so deleĉable to sit out of doors in the garden as it had been in the summer afternoons; the dark came sooner and allowed no evening outings; and worſt of all, the beginning of the war againſt Germany had brought upon everybody a gloom such as John Smith's health was by no means ſtrong enough to endure. Had he not lived too long? He said little: sat silent and mournful for long ſtretches. It was a mark of his depression, of his own weariness, when he observed, speaking of his dead siſter Ann, " I'm thankful poor old Auntie didn't live to see all this wickedness. 'Twould have diſtressed her so."

The time was indeed melancholy. On the second, or perhaps the third, day of his visit the morning papers were full of the " frightfulness " of the attack upon Antwerp; and as the day wore on a helpless indignation settled down on us all, the news growing blacker hour by hour. " Frightfulness " itself was a failure: it did not frighten, but filled one with shame, so that it was no longer decent to look upon the decencies of human nature. Such an attitude, so unlike John Smith's own, would have made it unseemly to listen to his old talk of comparatively kindly life, even if he had cared to tell; but he did not care. He sat quiet, low-spirited; as if feeling that his life had been a failure, that the world was foul. He went back home the next day; back to his sick-bed soon; and to the best of my belief he never got about again.

Now and then I went to see him. I had tea with him once upstairs in his bedroom, looking down across the quiet fields he had once farmed, and watching the unquiet aeroplanes that were now circling about over them. At my next visit his bed had been brought downstairs—it was easier for him and for everybody that he should be there. There he lay till the summer came round again, and flies from the farm-yard across the road were tiresome—lay in almost constant pain, but with serenity and humorous good-temper almost as constantly with him. His old acquaintances sometimes dropped in for a chat; for still it was worth while to listen to him. He had a laugh left.

It was with a laugh he told of a certain colonel he had known, retired colonels being thick as blackberries in that district, and well-nigh as

A Farmer's Life

unvalued. One such Mr. Smith had heard wondering how they milked cows into those tremendous high milk-churns you see at railway ſtations. Had military gentlemen been able to witness my uncle's amusement, they would have had uneasy doubts about the genuineness of the respeἃ generally shown to them in country places. I, for my part, had little doubt. Mr. Smith evidently had none too high an opinion of the common-sense of officers. Nor yet of officers alone. The pretensions of the classes they are drawn from—the gentry and their like—ſtruck him as comic. Such people muſt be humoured; yet a really praἃical man might smile to himself.

My uncle allowed his prejudices to carry him perhaps a little too far in this direἃion. In my laſt talk with him—he lay on his bed, feeble, helpless, and in pain—he spoke with his old humour of several ladies of the parish who were thinking to take up farm-work during the war. One of them had come to visit him—a nice cheery woman whose visits he appreciated, he said. But he had told her—and now with the old twinkle in his eyes he repeated to me:

" Yes, I think with cows you might do something—if there was about two others with ye, and somebody to clean out the cow-ſtall and get the fodder together and tie the cows up. Then I dessay you might milk one—or perhaps two

162

Collapse

after a time. . . . *I* kept at it when I was an old man, before this trouble crippled me. As long as I was able to get up nimble whenever a cow kicked me over I didn't mind. But when I found I had to lay there and she might step forward and tread on me, I had to give up."

So Mr. Smith, according to his own account. And the lady replied, " Oh ! do they kick you over when you are on the milking stool ? " My uncle laughed, telling me. His guest had seemed alarmed, and inclined to think again before offering her services to " her friend Lady So-and-so," to look after her four gentle Jerseys.

If Mr. Smith had lived to see what women accomplished in the war, he must have revised his opinion of them. It may, however, be observed, that he was only talking of one woman, in the idler classes. Moreover, he had nothing himself left to take pride in except his memories of his own lost prowess.

This was in the spring of 1915, and proved to be my last talk with him ; for he died in the summer of that year (July 10). Yet it was not the last time I saw him alive. The evening before his death I stood beside him, although he did not see me or seem to know that I was there. Now and again, in very feeble voice, he called out " Susie," and I suppose he was appealing to his sister, dead thirty years before, who

A Farmer's Life

had been once the mainstay of his family. Earlier in the day (they told me) he had called to his other dead sister, Ann; and once he had cried "Father." No doubt his dying memory had worked back to his childhood at Farnborough. . . .

Afterwards, along the road and between the fields where I had known him strong and able of course it seemed a loss that I should never again have that joy, and that the country of which he had seemed so integral a part should see him no more. Yet it was strongly borne in on me that death—his coming death—was not to be deplored, because it was in the natural sequence of good life. In my uncle's case the other stages had been good—the childhood and growing-up, the mature efficiency, the peaceful ageing—and now the end was quite in the appointed order. . . .

This sort of thought, most soothing, accompanied me along the towing-path of the canal through the summer evening; and the summer sights, so tranquil too, admitted my view of death into their company not at all as if death were opposed to them, but as if it were a completion of them. I have rarely seen so harmonious an evening. Sunny, warm, clear it was. High-coloured thundery clouds across the evening blue were reflected in the canal amidst the vivid green of the rushes. From the banks,

Collapse

where there were a few steel-blue dragon-flies, moorfowl now and then started out. The rushes clustered thick along the opposite bank; on the nearer side grasses stood tall—around alders and withies, while "skater" insects darted to and fro on the placid water. Here and there men and boys were fishing; there were a few men in khaki in boats, a few on the bank, and not many other people. But, as I caught the snatches of talk, and saw the signs of interest in the passing show of life, I felt that it was all as it should be. My uncle lay dying: he was going through his stage, even as these younger people were going through theirs and I through mine: and each, taking the stage that came, was doing well.

For a time I forgot the war, or, rather, was able to see it as but a passing incident in this larger, this perennial business of living and then dying. From the railway platform, while waiting for my train, I watched a distant ridge of the Fox Hills—the heath on them a very rich velvety green in the glowing evening sunlight. So silent, those hills looked; so enduring; so antique. And presently I was feeling how they might be standing there just so, thousands of years hence, when perhaps this bustle of English life has vanished clean away and left them alone again. And that too seemed part of a Programme. . . .

Chapter 22 *Souvenirs*

AMONGST numerous odds and ends
that awaken my memories of Farnborough or of the Smith family, I view
with some antiquarian sentiment a
genealogy of my grandfather, William Smith the
potter—John Smith's father. This genealogy
traces William Smith's anceſtry back to 1708, and
gives the date 1764 for the birth of his mother
—that "carnayin" old cottage woman shown
beside her hearth in the book about him. How
her maiden name was Ann Paige, how she was
married to Thomas Smith (my great-grandfather)
as a young woman of sixteen in 1780, and was
widowed twenty years afterwards, is of small
importance now or of none at all; and equally
unimportant is the nature of the document—its
odd spelling, its quill-pen writing—in which
these things are recorded. I cannot even surmise who wrote the record, or why it ſtops at
1805; and it is only of the very fainteſt intereſt,
and to me alone, that I may have seen one man
mentioned in this genealogy. Richard Young,
farmer at Ash, was certainly a very old man when
I knew him slightly, about 1886. He was a
man to be eſteemed—though by no means for
his wealth. Tall and ſtraight, very thin, grey-

haired, ruddy-cheeked, he was a fine specimen of a hard-working farmer; and I wish I had asked him whether it was true, as once or twice I heard, that he was somehow related to me. It can hardly have been though (now I come to consider it) that he was the Richard Young of this genealogy, born 1796—a cousin of my grandfather. Yet, if he was of a later generation, I am glad to have set eyes on him, glad to have known his mild, grey-eyed, almost apologetic manner. I think of him as a South-country illustration of those Scotsmen in Stevenson's verse, " Where the old plain men have rosy faces "; for that was the Richard Young I knew —probably a son of the man mentioned in William Smith's genealogy, and not the very man himself. Old, plain, rosy-faced, of sterling and quiet character, capable at all laborious farm-work, plainly he was contented to be a nobody as long as he could be it with dignity.

Bearing him in mind, I return to that genealogy to indicate the one point in it that takes hold of me—the connection of John Smith's ancestors with Ash. His great-grandparents belonged apparently to that parish: his grandfather, an Ash man, married a girl of the same village; and behold, in my own time, Richard Young, a cousin, turns up from Ash too.

What is there in it? Ash always struck me

A Farmer's Life

as a place to avoid, it had been so corrupted by
Aldershot. Two railway companies had eſtab-
lished pettifogging ſtations there, and the neighbourhood felt mean as well as ugly. But had it
always been so? I had, and I have, nothing at
all on which to form an opinion of its condition
in the eighteenth century; only, without the
camp, and without the railways, why should not
Ash have had its share of ruſtic comeliness? I
tried to imagine that crabbed old great-grand-
mother of mine as a young girl courting there.
Her family anyhow thought well enough of
themselves to keep a record of their births,
marriages and deaths—probably in a family
Bible; and though I knew nothing of their
ſtatus, I knew perhaps something of the family
charaćter; while here, helpfully, was Richard
Young in the flesh—juſtifying in himself all my
beſt dreams of the family, and offering, in his
own occupation, a hint of what theirs may have
been a century ago, before the neighbourhood
was spoilt. Ash became quite a decent place to
think of then.

With this came further light, as I fancy, on
John Smith's father and the ſtock he came from.
Though he had been brought up as a potter, his
family, on the father's side—provincials in the
beſt sense—had been of yeoman breed: pious,
induſtrious nobodies. They belonged to that

168

element of quiet strength in England which furnished no subjects for novels, no excitements for lawyer or judge or politician, no romance for poets, but kept the country orderly and industrious.

This aspect of England's career gathered for me around that genealogy, to suggest (when I was not at all looking for such a thing) a sort of social origin for John Smith's life. It linked him up with the rustic English, the able nobodies who had dwelt in their villages and mowed their hay and thatched their barns for centuries. He came from the procession of men who were emphatically the English—the men whose value Evelyn and Gilbert White and Arthur Young could appreciate. "Rosy-faced," thin, grey-eyed, quiet—they were perhaps more than a trifle slow of wit, not to say stupid; yet they knew England in all her fields—and not Gray in his *Elegy* spoke too highly of the sort of men they were. It cannot have been otherwise. Novelists may have left evil accounts of the eighteenth-century English; but you cannot have a John Smith with no traditions behind him; and when you see a man like Richard Young you may fairly discern in him what the character of his country-side must have been through many generations.

A different factor in my uncle's make-up is suggested by another memento. From the

A Farmer's Life

heaths and corn-fields and tree-lined lanes and
the courting couples of eighteenth-century Ash
—from this dream of rural England—imagination drifts off, I find (I only knew it on seeking
the cause of a certain vague change of sentiment
that had come over me for a second), to eighteenth-
century Westminster. A touch of old London
comes in—the London of John Gilpin. The
age-long country sleep is awakened by the chatter
of a City inn. A silver crown-piece I keep—a
five-shilling piece—is what does it. The coin,
to be sure, was minted in the sixteen nineties—
the last figure of its date has been worn down
smooth. Yet it bears another date. For all
across the image of King William III is engraved,
in careful writing, the following inscription:
" Susanah (*sic*) Blackburn Born 16th Decr 1794
given by R Martin Senr."

Who R. Martin, Senr. can have been it passes
me to say. I never heard of him in any other
connection; but surmise discovers in him an
esteemed crony of Mr. or of Mrs. Blackburn.
Now, the Susannah Blackburn of this gift was
—my own grandmother; and so, thanks to this
coin, I am reminded (almost unawares, as I have
hinted) of that other element which tinged and
probably invigorated the tradition in which John
Smith grew up. The provincial outlook remained. Through his father's family he received

Souvenirs

ſtrong ruſtic influences from the Ash anceſtry; but his mother's attitude could not fail to be affeẁed by the R. Martins or other seniors who had hobnobbed with her father and mother during her girlhood in London. As I look upon the coin the inn at Weſtminſter grows cloudy again with tobacco-smoke; shrewd talk, with plenty of common-sense, clatters across the rooms. It is gone now. It is nothing. And yet, did not that five-shilling piece ſtand for one of the influences that ſtill coloured Susannah Blackburn's behaviour at Farnborough years afterwards, when my uncle John Smith was a little boy? It suggeſts, to me, why he grew up a bit more nimble of wit than so many of his social equals; why a larger outlook than that of Farnborough swayed him; why he had the habit of looking at things from a national point of view. His mother was used to hearing talk of that charaẁer in the inn parlour down by the river, from men like R. Martin, Senr. who gave her this crown-piece. She amongſt the glasses heard it; a century later, echoes of similar talk reached myself in John Smith's chatter.

These things—the coin and the genealogy—had both been put away and I had forgotten them until this book was all but done. But in the meantime another souvenir with its own odd mode of suggeſtion had come into my hands.

171

A Farmer's Life

It came this way. My uncle made me one of the executors of his will, incidentally requesting me to make quite sure that he was not buried before he was really dead. That betrayed, indeed, a family fear. His father's burial had been deferred ten days or so; his two uncles had lain dead, I am told (they died of diabetes), each almost a month unburied. I was therefore not surprised at my uncle's request, and of course readily assented. Indeed, no reflection on his own sons and daughters was at all implied. John Smith was only indulging his taste for talking seriously and ceremoniously, while he paid me the compliment of admitting me, as it were, into the inner circle of his affections. That was the meaning of his odd request; and soon after his death I was allowed to feel it. Because of the close friendship between him and me, I was given a little book which he had treasured, in the belief that I should treasure it too.

I did. A duodecimo it was, long associated with John Smith's family—an account of the *Royal George* lost in 1782, and of the abortive attempts to " weigh the vessel up " in 1783. This tiny volume, published at Portsea by S. Horsey in 1843, was bound in thinnest boards of oak said to have been recovered (truly enough I dare say) from the sunk timbers. Tom Blackburn, a sailor, had given the little curiosity to his

172

Souvenirs

sister Susannah Blackburn; from her it passed to her son, the John Smith of this book; and in his keeping it had for years been a treasure—lying about, I understood, in window-sills, nor yet put away—perhaps because of a singular suggestiveness it has; a singular power to draw pleasant associations clustering round it.

At least this is what I myself experienced. Although the little volume was but too often something else to move where there was already too much, for weeks I could not bring myself to clear it off my table. Every time my sight happened upon it some agreeable fancy or other seemed to be stirred. Now I remembered the farm-house window it had lain in, and began fancying old-time haymakings or harvests. Now the black-brown oak-grain took my thoughts dreaming away to leafy forests two hundred years ago or so, and to sawyers and timber-carting: now sailor-men and the "wooden walls of old England" seemed to be recalled there. A curious thing was that thoughts of my uncle himself were not often wakened up in this way. The souvenir took me one or two generations farther back. The fancies it kindled epitomised so much of England's strong life that memories of John Smith himself seemed almost crowded out.

But it may be surmised that the effect was

really far more subtle. Instead of suggesting memory-pictures of my uncle himself, the book was causing my brain, my feelings, to do the same things that it had caused my uncle's brain, my uncle's feelings, to do long ago. A moment or two of his very life was repeated; at least closely enough to let me experience, in my own appreciations, how the world sometimes felt to John Smith.

Not that he was introspective. Only, if he had looked at his fancies (when this little volume sent its own peculiar light playing across them), would he not have enjoyed consciously delights that I too have since enjoyed? More vividly perhaps. The memories called up were, for me, of things only seen; but, for him, of things actually done. I had but looked on at the hay-makings, the timber-cartings; but he had taken his share in them. He was a partaker in that English life of which it had to suffice me to be a spectator. Even the ship-building which the book recalled was nearer to him, in point of time, than it was to me. He would have heard at school of "Lord Howe's Great Victory." From his mother he might know a thing or two about Nelson and catch echoes from old Westminster talk of the Navy. He had but to go to the Solent to see other ships like this *Royal George*, whose oak had furnished covers for the book now

174

on his window-sill. In short, he was very near to the England epitomised in the suggestions awakened by this volume. In his way he had been a part of it.

Therefore, as I have said, if the souvenir did not bring up pictures of himself to me, it did what was perhaps even better; giving me as it were his very eyes to look through; or, actually, quickening in my brain cell-motions very like his had been. For a moment, if no more, the mental activity was repeated: an old memory glistened, though in another mind.

Ann Smith
1831—1913

M

Ann Smith

I

FARMER SMITH'S third daughter Ann —" Aunt Ann " or " Auntie " to all the farmer's grandchildren—had been dead some years before it came home to me how much she muſt have suffered from noſtalgia in her long life. I ought to have known it. I ought to have underſtood, better than in faĉt I did, her eagerness to accept my siſters' offer to come and live with us for the reſt of her days. Inſtead of underſtanding it I thought her haſte almoſt indecent. It was not made known to me that she had, in faĉt, been careful to assure herself that she would not be intruding. I was not allowed to see any trace of hesitation. Within a fortnight she had finally left her own little house— so pleasant to her, I had thought—and had arranged for selling the furniture she did indeed prize ; and here she was, at her needlework—a fixture under my own roof. For years afterwards she continued here, one of the family (sometimes rather in the way, to tell the truth) ; and ſtill I was too dense to realise that she had, in faĉt, found with us something better than the refuge all old people ought to have.

But gradually it dawned on me that probably

A Farmer's Life

she had been a prey to a sort of home-sickness during many years; and that to come to this house as an inmate was, for her, something like coming home at laſt. It fed the hunger of years; it put an end to a heartache she had never grown quite used to.

It was in going mentally over her hiſtory that I began to see this, while I was writing the narrative of her father's life. Ann herself certainly never lamented; would have been grieved, or would have laughed perhaps, had anyone hinted that her life had ever been lonely. Nobody, and leaſt of all herself, thought her unhappy. She was as chirrupy as a bird. They say that as soon as she was awakened o' mornings she began chattering like a child—which is what she always was in temper—a seven-year-old in simplicity, no longer childish but childlike to the end. She never could believe that people liked to be alone sometimes—she had no need for solitude herself. Nor yet did it ever seem fit to her to be long without speaking, if there was anybody to speak to. That would have been to behave morosely, and morose she never was. As I say, she was a child in temper; a child of moſt sensitive affeċtion, knowing no place like home. Almoſt tragic was it, therefore, to be praċtically obliged to leave every place she could have looked upon as home for fifty or sixty years.

Ann Smith

She was apprenticed at fourteen years old (that would be in 1845) as a dressmaker under my father's sister Margaret in Farnham. The apprenticeship was for two years, and the premium thirty shillings. She was able every Saturday to go back to the old Farnborough home. A cart was usually sent to fetch her; but the farm business would not allow of such interruption to send her back on Monday mornings. She went back to her work by coach, the fare being eighteenpence for the journey—the seven miles. At Farnham she lived in lodgings, at Mrs. Frost's, somewhere in East Street. There one of her father's waggons coming for clay often brought food for her from the farm; but for the rest she was probably one of the family with her employer. The hours of work were from eight to eight; but in busy times they began at six. Truly she was proud of being Farmer Smith's daughter, so she laughingly told us in her old age; and once she was not a little indignant at a report that reached her, to her father's detriment, she thought. Another farmer, having come past the Farnborough farm or pottery, reported that " Farmer Smith was swearing at his men like anything." " So cruel," Ann thought it; " so cruel of Farmer Hall to say such a thing " of her father.

Certainly she herself, in all my memory of her, never spoke an unkind word about anyone but herself—unless once, in an impersonal way. This was when she mentioned—I forget in what connection—how much she had disliked to see the other dressmaking girls drop their work and begin to be idle as soon as my aunt Margaret's back was turned.

Amongst the treasures she brought with her when she finally came to this house was an old purse containing a few crooked sixpences. She had had a little hoard of them once—a couple of dozen or so. Her sister Susan had saved and given them to her, one at a time, on those Saturday returns from the apprenticeship to the farm home. After seventy years they still seemed to tell of sisterly love. It betokens that the elder sister considered often the other's plight, and that the younger knew and remembered the sympathy, with emotion on either side for which they had no words.

2

AFTER the apprenticeship was over, a weekly wage of three shillings was offered, but I think declined. Ann was twenty years old and at home again when that expedition was made to the Great Exhibition which Ann's father chose to think beneath an experienced man like himself. A party was made up from the two families—some Smiths from Farnborough, some Sturts from

Ann Smith

Farnham, with other friends too—and off they went by train to London. In the same compartment with them, and bound on the same errand, travelled a party of men from the Waverley Abbey estate near Farnham. At Ash these men began upon their food. They had brought with them a shoulder of mutton, and they cut their slices from it in the train. Did they pick the bone clean? At the Exhibition itself bones and refuse from other picnics lay about under the stalls. The Farnborough party travelled home in a cattle-truck—glad to secure even that, so crowded was the traffic.

Ann had always loved " treats," and no doubt the excitement of this excursion was a treat for her. Yet I surmise her daily life was happier if quieter during the few years of her life at home again, once the apprenticeship was done. Her own disposition must have assured that for her. As she was always quick to discern in ordinary people the underlying goodness, so in them the goodness started out to welcome her; and it was not wonderful if they liked her much. She by no means fancied that her own temper had anything to do with it. The people were amiable, or " nice," as she said. She found a little local work to do, and it's remarkable with what a number of " nice " acquaintances it brought her into contact.

183

A Farmer's Life

Thus there was Mrs. Jerome, at a certain turn-pike gate. Carrying her needlework to Frimley —Mrs. Cresswell's or Mrs. Burrell's—Ann had to pass the " pike," where dwelt Mr. Jerome, the keeper of it, a little short, very stout man. And his wife " was just such another," only more so. Such a nice kind woman. Invariably, after Ann had gone through, Mrs. Jerome had a bunch of flowers for her when she came back. Mrs. Cresswell was another who never let the dress-maker go away without flowers.

One odd thing occurred about the end of this period, or perhaps at some short return to it. The date can be fixed : it was the 17th of April, 1860 ; Ann's father being dead then and the Longmans being at Farnborough Hill. According to Ann's own memory it was at three o'clock on a May morning—probably she was a little wrong in her hour, as in her date, but evidently she was remembering a spring dawn in the old farm-house—when she, with my mother to help, had arisen to get on with some urgent needlework. As the two were settling down in the quiet bedroom and enjoying the early morning, suddenly the peace was broken by yells and hubbub growing into prolonged riot, from the Hatches—the meadows out Frimley way, just beyond the South-Eastern railway station. It was the noise of the crowds at the prize-fight between Sayers and

Ann Smith

Heenan in these meadows. The rabble was as on
Derby Day, with the heterogeneous crowds, the
innumerable vehicles. Bishops were said to be
there; special trains brought in throngs of specta-
tors. Indeed it was an Occasion. Long afterwards folk visited the spot, and even cut turf from
the ring to take away as a souvenir. The only
connection Street Farm had with it was lending
a towel for the prize-fighters; but old Mr. Longman was as pleased as anything to think that one
of his meadows had been the scene of such a
famous affair, Ann said. One of the kindest,
nicest of old men, she remembered him to have
been. When she had clean forgotten—if she
ever knew—who won the fight, she still recalled
Mr. Longman's grey head and mild, venerable
aspect.

3

It must have been soon after this that Ann
left her home again to live with my mother and
help with the young family of us, in Farnham.
Her presence, as one of the household, is a part
of my earliest recollections. Shall I ever forget
her cautionary tales? or, rather, shall I ever regain
them properly? One of them was all right: it
told how she, in her own childhood, had fallen
through the ice on a pond (Slade's Pond) she had
been forbidden to venture upon. But another

tale there was. Laughing, she disclaimed all knowledge of it in her old age, when I tried to tease her for having ſtuffed me up with hiſtory of a boy who broke his leg because he put matches under his pillow at night. Ann knew nothing about it; but the faƈt that she was associated with my memory of it shows how she had become bound up with my infancy. Truly, she was a second mother to us children at Farnham. Not that I, for one, cared. The arrangement muſt have laſted ten years or so; but I seem hardly to have noticed when it ended, and I never knew why. Want of bedrooms may well have obliged her to go; or perhaps want of family income. Anyhow, to me, self-centred little prig that I was, these matters were utterly unimportant. I only remember, now, that a time came when Aunt Ann was known to have gone as housekeeper to some ſtrange family at Sevenoaks, and I recall dimly having underſtood that she wasn't very happy there. I underſtood it to be a pity; for I don't think it was ever suggeſted that she met with anything but kindness, and it was unlikely to enter my head that a grown-up aunt might be homesick.

How many years this laſted I don't know. It came to an end dreadfully at laſt, and Ann had to go back to her old farm home, not now as a careless child.

Ann Smith

Her sister Susan had unexpectedly and without hope broken down, with cancer. For two years or so she had said nothing about it; she had kept the trouble to herself for all that time, hoping, so it was hinted to me, to spare her mother's old age that news. But eventually she could do no other than tell; and swiftly, after that, all her strength gave out—except, indeed, her courage to suffer.

So Ann came home, to be sick-nurse. I heard of dressings of the frightful wound. I only heard, but Ann actually went through it day after day for months—Ann, the sensitive, the tender-hearted—facing it as she had always faced trouble, without thought for herself. Inexperienced, she took on the sick-nursing; she also tried to be to her mother the support her dying sister had been. Of course the most arduous of Susan's duties had come to an end long ago. The pot-shop had been given up at William's death; John, married now, was able to manage the farm; and now Susan's own baking and her little grocery shop were perforce closed. In short, the old activities of Street Farm were dying out: a decrepit old age, as it were, was falling on the once busy household. Yet still there was much to do: the milk from the farm had to be got rid of daily: the house called for as much cleaning and scrubbing as ever, and the old mother—eager to be useful—needed care

187

herself, and probably caused more work one way than she saved another. And meanwhile the beloved sister lay upstairs, in pain and dying.

That Ann was overwrought was never said, in my hearing. Yet it may be suspected, from one circumstance that was told, was whispered rather, afterwards. I give it from hearsay, for she never spoke of it to me. A night or two before Susan's death, her wraith had been met by Ann on the stairs, or a formless figure had been seen by her at the foot of the bed. I don't know which it was; but Ann never doubted it. She was no spiritualist; on the other hand, she had no psychology to guard her against what her own weary brain might do. She told piteous things about her sister's death, tender things about the thoughtful kindness the Longmans at Farnborough Hill showed to the dying woman. The death happened in October 1881, Susan being then about fifty-eight years old.

The old mother, with Ann to take care of her, remained at the farm another year and a half. She had spent over sixty years there. Then she too died (February 1883), being about eighty-five years old; and once more Ann was without a home.

4

For though John, who had been running the farm for his mother, moved into the house, he

Ann Smith

didn't keep it on. He took a larger farm and another house at Frimley; and Ann went to live at Brixton with her youngest sister, Mary, married to a builder there. By and by, the builder dying and leaving Mary all but penniless (he had been speculating heavily), these two sisters had to work for their living again. Mary, it's true, had the house they lived in—it was mortgaged, I fancy—and was at least nominally the mistress, though there was no feeling of superiority or inferiority between the sisters. They took life laughingly and good-humouredly; they liked their lodgers and were liked by them. Only, the builder's debts were now his widow's; and the worry and anxiety arising from them preyed upon her so, that after some years—I have no dates—she developed heart trouble and soon died. So there was Ann (who had played sick-nurse now for the third time—first to Susan, then to her mother, and now to Mary) left alone again. And the family was dwindling fast. She had no sister left—my mother at Farnham was dead—and there was but one brother left alive—John, at Frimley. Both he and Ann were getting on in years too.

What was Ann to do? She couldn't stay in Brixton; the old house at Farnborough had been given up; she had next to no property—about ten shillings a week was her income. She was too old for employment; and now she was home-

189

A Farmer's Life

less. It was John (" Jacky," she always called him) who came to the rescue. I think his own wife was dead, and a daughter was keeping house for him. But at cost of some inconvenience, and perhaps some anxiety (for Ann was now old enough yet active enough to be interfering), John found room for her in his farm-house at Frimley. There she dwelt—offering more help, I fancy, than was always desired—until a chance occurred, and she took it, to rent a small cottage for herself in Farnham.

5

THE Farnham cottage was just across the street from the workroom of her apprenticeship days— my own office by this time; but the attraction to Ann was probably in being within walking distance—just over a mile, in fact—from this place where my sisters lived with me. We had always been as children to her; and now, at last, after a quarter of a century or so, she was near us again. Besides, she saw me almost daily. Usually I called on her o' mornings, and sat smoking—she loved me to make myself at home—in her little kitchen, watching the preparations for her own and her lodger's dinner. Sometimes I strolled out with her into her little back garden, and had her plants pointed out to me. Always if possible I had tea with her, she being careful to give me the warmest side of the fire. In course of time, too,

190

Ann Smith

I got the habit of playing a game at cribbage with
her before going home. I didn't altogether like
going away and leaving her to a lonely evening.
The cribbage lasted just long enough. The end
of a game was a signal that I must go now. Moreover, I had often nothing to say and I welcomed
the cards.

Another great point about this cottage was that
it was her very own home. Never before had
she been mistress in her own place; but now. . . .
Yes, she enjoyed it. Once or twice she hired a
small girl or boy to help at her rougher work, but
as far as her strength allowed she did all the work
herself. Sometimes I fell in with her along the
street. Being a little near-sighted, she walked
peeringly with her head bent slightly down to see
the pavement better; and, whether or no the shop-
keepers liked her, she certainly liked them, talking appreciatively of Mr. Hawkins, the butcher,
Mrs. Vass, who sold tea at a little sweet-shop near
her, and of others. It was her way to like people.
I remember her laughing about a certain farmer
who delivered a fowl at her door. Mrs. Smith,
he called her. She told him she was Miss.
" Oh ! You be one of 'em ? " he said, and then
took pains to reassure her : he knew numbers of
estimable single women, and thought none the
worse of her for being unmarried.

One of her delights at this cottage was in being
able to give parties herself. Now and again the

A Farmer's Life

whole family of us would have to assemble there to tea—even to supper—all of it made ready by her own hands; and we played cards in the intervals. A party of this kind was going on when the news of Queen Victoria's death was brought in. It quenched our gaiety, stopped our whist. Soon we all went home. Oftener she had visitors—friends from Brixton spending a day or two with her, or relatives from Farnborough calling for an hour; and in these latter cases she loved to talk of old times and to tell of her childhood.

A very dear caller was her own brother John. He used to look me up in my office, then hobble across the street (corns crippled him; he was ruptured too) to see " Aunt Ann." Once when he came in—it was about half-past twelve—I invited him to walk home with me presently for dinner.

" I've just arranged to have dinner with your aunt Ann," he said.

" Go and see if you can't come with me instead. I'll be over myself in about ten minutes."

In ten minutes I crossed the street and found him sitting by the fire. The table was laid for two. Aunt Ann entered the room, and, for her to hear, I repeated my invitation to her brother.

" No," he said; " thank you. I'll stay here now, and come out to you for tea."

" But would you sooner go out now?" Ann

192

asked. "Because, if you would—of course, I'm pleased to have you—but . . ."

He interrupted, declining my invitation once more. So Ann bustled out again to her kitchen, and John said to me, cautiously, "It'd suit me ever so much better to come with you; but I can see she won't like it if I do."

"Well, then I shall see you later? I must just go and say good-bye to her." I went out into the kitchen.

She whispered, "Is he going to stay?"

"Yes."

"I rather wish he'd go with you—for I haven't got much of a dinner. . . ."

It was during this period that I took to making notes of the frequent talks I heard about the old farm at Farnborough. But meanwhile Ann was getting older. Others—never herself—began wondering what was to become of her; and there may have been some anxiety of her own at the back of her readiness to come, as I have told, to live permanently in my sisters' care under my own roof. At any rate she came; and that was the end of her wanderings, her homelessness. Once here, she put aside all anxieties: she was cheerful, laughing, talkative, a happy child again; busy with her needlework, busy with a special bit of garden given over to her. Sometimes she would try to read; but she hadn't got the habit and her sight was none too good; and usually she

was more ready for a game at cribbage than for a
book. Yet, if anyone would read to her, she
preferred that even to cards. *Esmond* was a
special delight to her. My sisters introduced
her to many books on that level; and once, when
she had to keep her bed for a few days and I read
The Pilgrim's Progress to her, her happy appreciation greatly enhanced the value of that book for
me.

Old Farnborough days were never far from her
thoughts. Without her insisting on them or
being troublesome about them at all, the memories
seemed to spring, like daisies from a lawn, out of
her smooth daily doings. Often there was a
little whimsical laugh in them at her own expense.
Thus she was amused to tell how, once, she stole
an orange from her mother's cupboard, peeled
it, and then, overtaken too soon by conscience,
put it back where she found it. It was its own
evidence against her; but that was a consideration
that at no time of her life had any weight with
Ann Smith. Once a course seemed right to
her she followed it. And, as her conscience
had nothing else to worry about, it sometimes
exercised itself over childish peccadilloes. " It
troubles me now," she said one day, having
related some momentary passion of contempt she
had given way to all alone, over a small kindness
of her mother's for which she felt she was too
old. After seventy years still she grieved.

Ann Smith

Not that she was strait-laced. She had no theories of Right and Wrong. Principles consciously formulated troubled her not at all. It was by a quicker insight she lived. Kindness and truthfulness stimulated in her an emotion—it hardly amounted to a sentiment—which saw in a flash the decent thing to say, to do, to think at any given moment; and she said it, did it, thought it, without hesitation.

So, as I say, she was nowise strait-laced, but quietly happy, and amused at her own little back-slidings. One New Year's Day she made a good resolution—to go to bed by ten o'clock every night. But ten o'clock found her at cribbage; so that by the end of January she was lamenting that she had not once kept her new rule. Two or three nights later she announced, with a mischievous smile, that she had decided to alter her good resolution. Henceforth she wouldn't go to bed until *after* ten. And to that she was able to keep.

Perhaps she was not singular in this respect, yet I feel that the memories of childhood were unusually near the surface in her case. Truly, the years had not robbed her of her innocence. I have seen her throw herself back in her arm-chair to laugh, with the mischievous gaiety of six years old. However that may be, one never foresaw what touch of other days was coming from her. A baby boy from a neighbouring cottage was the

195

A Farmer's Life

subject of her child-fancies. What old nursery rhymes was she not going to teach him? Her own death, long before he was ready, intervened; but amongst other things he was to learn her own child-names for the thumb and fingers—Tommy Tomkins, Mary Molkins, Long Sarah, Sukey Salkins, and Little Frisk-about. So the eighteenth century, it may be, was to pass a pleasant memory on to the twentieth. Of her old home-places Ann never tired of thinking. For instance, she told affectionately of a certain white rose, trailing over the trellis-work at the glass doors at the back of the farm sitting-room; then of the little grass-plot beyond, with a border of lilac round it. In this hedge was another rose, "a small cabbage-rose" no bigger over than a penny-piece, "but as double . . . and smelt so sweet!"

It may be this rose pleased her the more by being small, for that was another childlike trait in her—she liked the daintiness, as of toys, of small things. Only one flower appealed to her so strongly as the pimpernel—the wild heartsease. She would often stop to exclaim about it: partly, I always thought, because it copied the cultivated flowers so faithfully yet in less than a quarter of their dimensions. "Jack-jump-up-and-kiss-me" was her old country name for it.

And out of her daily doings further memories

Ann Smith

welled up. During a discussion about some needlework measurements she sat one day in unwonted silence, tightening her pocket-handkerchief round her wrist. Then she held out the measurement thus obtained. " That's six inches," she said. On its being tested with a tape it proved to be six and a quarter inches; but the folk method of measuring was none the less acceptable; it seemed so suggestive of old workrooms and old devices for meeting long-forgotten difficulties. With a sentiment of affection—because her mother had been wont to do just that thing in the old home at Farnborough, where also her father had done it " for luck " as long ago as she could remember—she hung a bunch of hops year by year in her little sitting-room at Farnham. But without any such reminder in my house, she seemed to be always recalling, and always happily, the farm and her young days. One early July, after a prolonged rain, she repeated the ancient village jest that the rain would spoil all the little potatoes—by " turning 'em into big 'uns ! " " I wonder how many people have been saying that this morning ! " she exclaimed, in a sort of quiet merriment. Were not the far-off, easy-hearted days still alive in her ? One had that feeling. She must have been thinking of her father. And in fact a perpetual recollection of the older time seems to have run through her brain, in never-ending comment on modern

A Farmer's Life

sights or sounds. Nor was the comment always unconscious or even silent. The least little thing would set her off. The sight of a road-man wearing a too large hat reminded her first of her father's beavers, and then prompted her to tell how she herself, in all her life, had never worn hat at all. When she was a little child her head-gear was a close-fitting quilted bonnet made of patchwork by her mother, and covering her ears ; and from then onwards she had always worn bonnets.

All sorts of details about her young days came to light in this fashion. Something in the street drew from her the exclamation, " What a long time ago it is since I saw a waggon with three horses in a long team in front of it ! "—from which it was plain to me that she was seeing again in memory her father's team taking pots to London. Another day the same memory brought with it, further, how Mrs. Stonehouse, wife of the vicar of Frimley, pleased her by speaking of " your father's beautiful team."

Old Farnborough village lived still in her memory, as it was in her childhood, ere ever the aircraft factory changed its character, and before ex-Empress Eugénie came to Farnborough Hill. Ann Smith told, rather, of Lady Palmer's small house lower down ; and of course she knew of the coming of the Longmans. The Longmans, newly arrived, introduced the Christmas tree to the parish. They made it the centre of a village festivity, everybody being invited and receiving a present from a huge Christmas tree at the big house.

So Ann told; yet oftener went back to everyday matters of her childhood. Once she dwelt lovingly on the old church in Farnborough Park, and especially the charm of its chancel. Over the communion-table—which was just a simple square table with a cloth on it—was, in place of the ordinary East window of modern church architecture, a long window with diamond-paned lead lights. Greenish but transparent glass showed the ivy that was creeping over from the outside wall; and beyond, the trees and the sky could be seen. The pews in the church were high and roomy. Mr. Morant's pew had no curtains, but was upholstered with green baize.

Another time she told of Slade's Pond—that roadside pond she passed every day on her way to school—the pond mentioned elsewhere in connection with Welsh cattle. Frosty weather made Ann Smith's memories of it vivid again; for once more she seemed to be a school-girl, watching her father, with several other leading men in the village, sliding on the pond. It was not generally deep—waggons went through it in dry weather—but a stream ran through it so that there had to be a pen-stock at one end; and here and in one other spot—" between the Island and the Hedge "—

199

there was deepish water. On this account, and because Slade's Pond was attractive during frosts, Ann was forbidden, as already told, to venture on ice there herself. There it was, accordingly, that she paid the penalty of disobedience, and fell through the ice into the water. But the mishap enriched her after all with a cautionary tale she never could tell too often. I do not remember hearing it for the first time. From my infancy I seem to have known " how Aunt Ann fell in the pond."

She had a quaint, mischievous manner, truly endearing, of " getting at," " chipping " people she liked. A friend of mine had been talking, with over-emphasis, of some practice or other which seemed to him to stamp the " High Church " with absurdity. Ann demurely let him finish, then, with a gleam in her eyes, turned to him, saying, " You know, I'm a bit High Church myself." It was most comic to see him look so flabbergasted ; yet he grew the more fond of her from that moment, she had done it so neatly, and the two always teased one another afterwards. As for her being " High " or " Low " Church, I never knew it. She was a devout churchwoman always.

Me too she honoured with an annual teasing. As sure as my birthday came round she had a little present for me, accompanied as surely with an affectionate note beginning " Dear *old* George."

Ann Smith

It amused her to rub it in that I was getting on in years; the fact was a joke between us that never failed. For her good-temper never failed—her affection.

A member of my household, to tease her one day, sighed audibly for some retreat " on a mountain, where there was no work to do." This was said with a fairly obvious intention of provoking a reproof from Aunt Ann, and hearing what she would say.

And the reproof came, very gentle. Quite sincerely Ann said, " No. I like work. I like to have something to do. And I like to feel that it's wanted—not to be doing it for the pleasure of being doing something."

She was eighty-two then; and then, as always, she had no thought of reward for her doings. To be knitting a woollen hearth-rug ; to help at washing-up the plates and dishes ; to be at needlework (rarely for herself), was her pastime up to the last week of her life. It kept her " in the swim " with all that she found best in human nature.

She died the 5th of August, 1913—just a year before the war began. And, as that calamity went on from horror to horror, her brother John, soon to die himself, expressed thankfulness (I have told it before) that " poor old Auntie " (as he called her to us) had been spared those evil days ; she would have been so distressed.

Appendix

NOTE A (p. 22)

IN his account of Maidstone and District, Marshall writes :

" No district in the Island, perhaps, of equal extent and fertility, breeds fewer cattle than the district under view. Its entire stock may, with little licence, be said to be Welch, or of Welch origin ; although it is situated at an extreme point of the Island, some hundred miles distant from the source of the breed. . . .

" The Welch cattle are mostly brought in, by drovers of Wales, while young ; as one, two, or three years old. They are bred in different parts of the Principality. But the heifers, which are brought in for milk, are mostly of the Pembroke-shire mould. Many of them make handsome cows, which are said to milk well, and to fat quickly. Several thousands, of different descriptions, are annually brought into the county. In the month of October the roads are everywhere full of them : some going to the upland districts, others to the Marshes."

(Marshall's *Rural Economy of S. Counties*, 1798, Vol. I.)

202

Appendix

Note B (p. 119)

The Glossary at the end of Best's *Rural Economy in Yorkshire* gives the following:

" *Caving Rake.* A barn-floor rake, used to separate (cave) the husks from the grain."

Parish's *Dictionary of the Sussex Dialect* gives:

" *Cavings* [*ceaf*, Ang.-Sax., chaff]. The short straws or ears which are raked off the corn when it is thrashed."

Note C (p. 155)

This tale of the man who crawled back into the ditch rather than owe any benefit to an enemy seemed to me authentic enough until I read the same tale, not from Farnborough, but from Ulster. Then I recognised its nature. It is one of a number of provincial or folk-tales, such as Englishmen have long loved to attach to some neighbour or other, either in derision of him, or in picturesque illustration of a well-known foible. The tale of the doctor whose pestle talked to his mortar is almost certainly another of the series. To be sure, I never heard it elsewhere; yet plainly it could be fitted to any country practitioner, and no less plainly a certain sort of Englishman would enjoy fitting it. In short, these stories have a quality hard to describe, perhaps, but very

Appendix

recognisable to any truly provincial Englishman. Others may fail to see it; but a native will feel it "in his bones."

Characteristic of all these is the tale of Cocker Nash (pronounced Naish)—to give the West Surrey version. It is told that Cocker Nash, a fish-hawker, being the worse for drink, lost his way in the woods of Waverley one winter evening; and, growing frightened, began to call out "Man lost! Man lost!" Pigeons said "Coo-oo, coo-oo." Was it an answer? Again the man cried; and again came the supposed answer. And now there could be no doubt: it must be some voice asking "Who? who?" Whereupon, almost frantic, the fishmonger screamed out, "Cocker Nash, of Farnham."

I think no other memory of Cocker Nash survives in Farnham, although it may be taken for granted that a simpleton of that name once lived there. Anyhow, the story is handy. My old friend Bettesworth once tried to fasten it on to a neighbour whose name must not be told; and indeed the narrative is a cap easily fitted. It is placed in Wessex by Mr. Hardy; some years ago a friend came upon it at Freshwater in the Isle of Wight, where the adventure was ascribed to a local worthy lost in the Undercliff. There is a version of it, again with a local name, at Dunstable; finally, I may mention a North-

Appendix

country variant, which tells, not of a man lost, but of a bachelor withdrawing to a wood to pray for a wife. " Who ? who ? " the voice seemed to ask ; and the answer was given, " Any wife will do, Lord ; any wife will do."

Pigeons figure in another story of this class ; and with a voice nowise attributed to the Lord. A certain Taffy (I don't know why he was a Welshman, but Richard Jefferies gives it so) went to steal a cow from a stall. Near the door hung a cage containing a pigeon or dove, usually saying nothing but " Coo-oo." But when the thief opened the door to take the cow—what was that ? A wicked, insinuating voice saying, " Take two, take two-o-o." Surely it was the devil, tempting the thief to double his crime ? But Taffy, thoroughly frightened, fled without a cow at all.

In *The Scouring of the White Horse* Thomas Hughes told how one Job Cork, in great trouble, was enjoined by his wife to " Ha' patience and think o' thy namesake," but retorted with a groan, " Ah, but he never had his breeches all cockled up "—for that was Job Cork's trouble. His chamois-leather breeches, wet through after game-beating, had been too quickly dried in the domestic oven, and proved unwearable in the morning. Precisely this was said to have happened to a neighbour of my own, in West Surrey.

205

Appendix

True, his name did not fit; but his wife did not fail, in the story, to bid him have patience and think of Job. I suspect that a certain yarn from Scotland (quite unprintable) is akin to this. The incident is different: Job is not mentioned; yet the old heartless rustic humour sounds clear in the wife's retort bidding her husband " Have patience " amidst his wailings under ridiculous misfortune.

In this sort of folk-anecdote there is enough of John Smith's whimsical humour, and of the country he belonged to, to justify, I hope, collecting further examples here. Moreover, it should be noted, these tales are rapidly dying out. The schoolmaster, the railway, the week-end cottage, are wiping away many such traces of an older England—wiping them clean away. So that if they are worth saving at all, that task cannot be undertaken too soon.

Some of the tales must be very old indeed. One there was, of which I remember a variant in Grimm's *Fairy Tales*. The hero there was, I think, a Prince, while the villain was a giant. In the English version (which reached me from Farnborough, but had probably come from Yorkshire) the persons were a small boy named Jack, and a chimney-sweep who had kidnapped him and carried him away in a sack. Crossing a heath, the sweep sat down and went to sleep. Jack crept out

Appendix

of the sack and put stones in, to take his own place. But the sweep said, " Jack, how heavy you be ! " and got the little boy into the sack again. Next time, Jack, thinking to escape detection, put in bushes instead of stones ; but it was no use. " Jack, how you pricks ! " said the sweep. So it came to a third occasion, when Jack put horse-droppings into the sack. Was this also a failure ? I do not know. The story ends with the sweep complaining, " Jack, how you stinks ! "

There is an old story of a London cabman called out from a public-house he had entered, by a boy : " Hi ! mister ! Your hoss is fell down ! " To which the cabman replied, indignantly, " Gahn ! You pushed him down ! " But Bettesworth knew this horse-driver by name. He was not a London cabman, but a West Surrey coal-hawker, and the horse was an ancient grey.

Many years ago a certain farmer in West Surrey had the reputation of being an atheist ; of whom the following incident was told, with something of a shudder. It was a wet hay-making ; the cut grass was spoiling in the meadows, and this impious man, taking some of it on a prong and holding it skywards, said contemptuously, " There, God ! What d'ye think o' that ? "

An impecunious young gentleman of Farnham who liked to be taken for a keen hand and a sportsman was generally alleged to have gone shooting

Appendix

duck at Frensham Pond, when he found too late that, instead of wild duck, he had been killing tame ducks, the property of the landlord of the inn, and that he would have to pay dear for his sport.

Tales of moon-rakers should be collected, and the history of moon-raking villages should be investigated, as an interesting feature in English country life. But this is not quite the place for discussing that matter. The subject of provincial folk-tales should not be left, however, without drawing attention to a curious anecdote— not quite of the humorous rustic order, yet obviously of traditional value. It is the tale of a missing will, discovered to the interested parties just in the nick of time, by the ghost of somebody long dead. The odd thing is the use to which this tale has been put. Sir Oliver Lodge (in *The Survival of Man*) gives it, without suspicion, as an authentic German occurrence proving spirit-life after death. But readers of *The Antiquary* may recall that Sir Walter Scott had told practically the same tale long before, giving it only a different setting.